CATS

S E Y M O U R   S I M O N

Smithsonian | Collins

An Imprint of HarperCollinsPublishers

Photo credits: p. 2: © Reed / Williams / Animals Animals; p. 3: © Al Cetta; p. 4: © Robert Maier / Animals Animals; p. 5: © Friedrich Von Horsten / Animals Animals; p. 6: © Roger Wood / Corbis; p. 7: © Renee Lynn / Photo Researchers; p. 8: © 1993 Ron Kimball / Ron Kimball Photography, Inc.; p. 9: © Agence Nature / Photo Researchers; p. 10: © Martin Harvey / Gallo Images / Corbis; p. 11: © Alan Carey / Photo Researchers; p. 12: © Robert Maier /Animals Animals; p. 14: © 1994 Margaret Miller; p. 15: © Renee Stockdale / Animals Animals; p. 16: © Carolyn A. McKeone / Photo Researchers; p. 17: © Grace Davies / Grace Davies Photography; p. 18: © 2000 Ron Kimball / Ron Kimball Photography; p. 19: © Grace Davies / Grace Davies Photography; pp. 20–21:© Fred Whitehead / Animals Animals; p. 22: © 1994 Margaret Miller; p. 23: © 1993 Margaret Miller; p. 24: © Marcia Griffen / Animals Animals; p. 25: © Renee Stockdale / Animals Animals; p. 26: © Henry Ausloos / Photo Researchers; p. 29: © Al Cetta; p. 30: © Henry Ausloos / Animals Animals; p. 31: © Grace Davies / Grace Davies Photography; p. 32: © Roy Morsch / Corbis

The name of the Smithsonian, Smithsonian Institution and the sunburst logo are registered trademarks of the Smithsonian Institution. Collins is an imprint of HarperCollins Publishers.

Cats

For information address HarperCollins Children's Books, a division of HarperCollins Publishers,
10 East 53rd Street, New York, NY 10022. www.harpercollinschildrens.com

Library of Congress Cataloging-in-Publication Data
Simon, Seymour.
    Cats / by Seymour Simon
       p. cm.—(Smithsonian)
    ISBN 978-0-06-173043-6 (trade bdg.) — ISBN 978-0-06-446254-9 (pbk.)
    1. Cats—Juvenile literature. [1. Cats.] I. Title.
SF445.7.S58 2004   2003008337
599.75—dc21   CIP
                                                                              AC

11   12   13   SCP   10   9   8   7   6   5   4   3   2
❖
Updated Edition

To Joyce and the feral cats who became our pets:
Mittens and Sir Isaac Newton (Newty Frewty)

Special thanks to Dan Wharton, Director, Central Park Zoo,
Wildlife Conservation Society, for his expert advice and to Don E. Wilson,
Senior Scientist, National Museum of Natural History, Smithsonian
Institution, for his invaluable contribution to this book.

Smithsonian Mission Statement

For more than 160 years, the Smithsonian has remained true to its mission, "the increase and diffusion of knowledge." Today the Smithsonian is not only the world's largest provider of museum experiences supported by authoritative scholarship in science, history, and the arts but also an international leader in scientific research and exploration. The Smithsonian offers the world a picture of America, and America a picture of the world.

All cats are hunting animals. They use claws and teeth to seize their prey. When you watch a cat play with a ball or a piece of yarn, it is almost like watching a tiger or a leopard stalking its prey in the wild. Even well-fed pet cats will try to catch mice or birds or insects.

Cats are great fun to watch. They make good pets, but they do not act at all like dogs. Dogs are noisy, friendly, and lively. Cats are quiet. They may disappear for hours without your being able to find them. But cats can also be friendly and will sit on your lap purring contentedly while you stroke their fur. Learning about cats can help you select your pet cat and take better care of it.

More than a hundred thousand years ago, wild cats were domesticated for the first time. About five thousand years ago, cats were used in Egypt to protect stored grain from mice and other rodents. Early Egyptians considered cats sacred animals. When a cat died, there was a period of mourning. Then the cat was mummified and buried in a casket in a cat cemetery. In one ancient Egyptian cat cemetery, more than 300,000 cat mummies were found.

From Egypt, pet cats began to spread across Asia and Europe. In Siam (Thailand today), only the king and royal family owned cats. The Siamese cat was the royal cat of Siam. By the Middle Ages, cats had become very popular in France and England. In the 1600s, they came to the Americas with the colonists. Nowadays, pet cats live with people in countries around the world.

Cats are not very big. Adults usually weigh between six and fifteen pounds. Cats have slim and flexible bodies. They can twist their bodies in amazing ways. The bones in a cat's back are much more loosely connected than the bones in your back. This makes a cat's body very bendable.

Cats are great climbers and jumpers. They also use their tails for balance. When a cat jumps, its body uncoils like a spring. A cat absorbs the landing shock easily with its front legs and the cushioning pads on its front paws. When a cat falls several feet, it twists its body in midair and lands on all fours, usually without hurting itself. This may be why people sometimes say a cat has nine lives.

Some people think that cats can see in the dark. Cats have excellent vision, but even they can't see in total darkness. They *can* see in light that is only one sixth as bright as the light humans need for seeing.

Cats have a special mirrorlike surface in the back of the eye called the *tapetum*. Faint light passes through the eye and then is reflected by the tapetum back out of the eye. The reflected light is what makes cats' eyes gleam in the dark and helps them see better at night.

Cats can see in color, but it doesn't mean much to an animal that hunts at night. Color plays no part in hunting a mouse in dim light or in deciding to nuzzle against your red shirt rather than your blue one.

Cats also have a good sense of hearing. They can hear sounds that are too soft or too high-pitched for humans to hear. A cat turns its ears very quickly to locate the direction of a sound. Hearing helps cats hunt for mice and other little animals when they move about.

A cat's whiskers are very sensitive to touch. Cats have whiskers on the chin, over the eyes, and on the backs of the front legs—not just on the upper lip. In the dark, whiskers help a cat sense objects that it cannot see. But it is not true that a cat's facial whiskers are exactly equal to the width of a cat's body.

Smell is another important sense in cats. Cats often will not eat food that has turned stale because of its bad odor. Cats have about nineteen million "smelling" nerve endings in their noses. Humans have only about five million. Cats love the smell of a plant called catnip. They sometimes roll around in catnip making happy sounds.

Cats are fussy eaters. Dogs will eat almost anything you give them off the table, but cats are much pickier. They don't have a "sweet tooth" and won't eat cookies or candy bars the way that dogs will.

If you have a pet cat, you may have tried to train it not to scratch the furniture. You may even have tried to teach your cat not to bring a dead mouse into the house. But a cat doesn't seem to learn these simple household rules. Does that mean that a cat is stupid or has a poor memory?

Neither is true. Cats learn and remember those things that are useful to them but not necessarily useful to you. It quickly remembers the location of the food and water dishes and the litter box. A cat even seems to remember its own name at mealtimes when it is called.

Cats remember things in their neighborhoods that they want to avoid, like a pesky dog. They may even remember where they live if taken away from home. But only with skillful training will a cat remember what YOU want it to remember.

Cats can't talk using words the way people do. But cats make sounds that tell you or other cats how they're feeling or what they want. Cats purr, gurgle, meow, wail, hiss, screech, and growl. Each of these sounds means something different.

Purring usually means everything is fine. Kittens purr to their mothers, and mothers purr to their kittens. Adult cats purr to each other when they are peaceful. Cats purr when you pet them. Gurgling is another happy sound cats make. Sometimes a cat will gurgle and meow for minutes in a kind of "cat  chat" with another cat.

A kitten meows if it is cold or lost or wants to be fed. Adult cats meow if they are hungry or unhappy about something. Hissing, screeching, and growling are angry sounds. The awful screech a tomcat makes at night is a cry of warning to other tomcats in the area to keep away from a female cat.

Cats also use body language to show what they are feeling. When a cat rubs itself against your legs or against another cat, it is happy and affectionate. If a cat points its ears forward, it signals friendly interest and watchfulness. An angry cat raises its ears and points them backward, narrows its eyes to slits, and pushes its whiskers forward. A cat that is hunting or playing opens its eyes wide, perks up its ears, and bristles its whiskers. When a cat is petted and happy, it partly closes its eyes and relaxes its body and whiskers.

When a cat arches its back, flattens its ears, and shows its teeth, the cat is afraid and defensive. If a cat is frightened, its hair stands up all over and its tail goes down. If it's about to pounce or attack, its hair stands up along the spine and tail. The tail whips from side to side or suddenly stands up.

There are many different ways that a cat "talks." Watch your cat carefully and you'll soon be able to figure out what each sound and body movement mean.

By the time they are a year old, female cats can have babies. After mating with a male cat, a mother cat will give birth to a litter of kittens in about sixty-five days. A litter can contain as many as a dozen kittens. The average litter is four kittens.

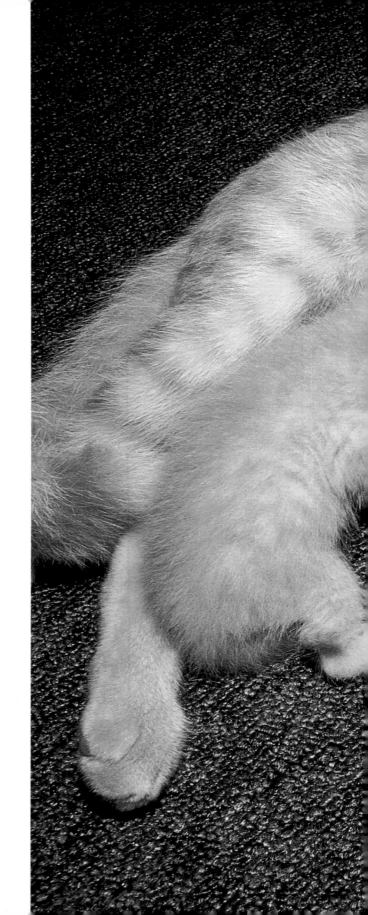

Kittens are usually born from five minutes to two hours apart. A kitten is born in a cloudy white sac filled with fluid. The mother licks each newborn kitten, breaks the sac, and removes the fluid from its face. Licking makes the kitten start to breathe.

The mother also bites through the *umbilicus* (the cord that carried food to the fetus and took away its waste while it was inside the mother). Even a first-time mother cat seems to know exactly what to do.

Right away, the newborn kittens suckle milk from their mother. She purrs and nuzzles them as they feed.

A newborn kitten is mostly helpless. Its eyelids are closed. Its ears are laid back. The tiny kitten can't see or hear. It weighs only two to five ounces. It's only about as long as a pencil. At birth, a kitten can wriggle and squirm, but it cannot walk.

Newborns snuggle together for the first week or so. The mother licks her kittens often. She carries them gently but firmly by the scruff of the neck. The mother and the babies soon learn to recognize one another by smell.

About eight days after birth, a kitten begins to open its eyes. In less than three weeks, it can see and hear.

A one-month-old kitten runs around and plays. It can weigh between nine ounces and eighteen ounces, which is just over one pound. By the end of its second month, a kitten eats solid food and has stopped nursing. A four-month-old kitten is completely independent of its mother.

Over the last century, people have developed more than one hundred different varieties of cats, called breeds. A cat can be a purebred or mixed-breed cat. Purebred cats are usually divided into two groups: longhaired cats and shorthaired cats.

The most popular breed of longhaired cat is called a Persian, or simply longhair. A Persian's fur is soft and may grow as long as five inches. It has a sturdy body, a round face, a short nose, round eyes, and short legs. A Persian's fur can be black, white, red, blue, smoky, tortoiseshell, calico, pewter, chocolate, or other color combinations.

Persians are usually quiet, even-tempered cats. That makes them ideal pets for people who keep their cats indoors.

Other longhaired cats, such as the Angora or the Balinese cat, have slimmer bodies and are more active than Persians. They are gentle, friendly, and playful.

A feral cat is a house cat that has gone back to being wild. For a feral cat living in a city or a big cat in the wild, having short hair can be an advantage. That's because long hair can get tangled in things when a cat is stalking its prey. Long hair also gives a cat's enemy something to grab on to. Shorthaired cats are far more common in nature than longhaired ones.

There are many kinds of purebred shorthaired cats, including British shorthairs, American shorthairs, Siamese, Manxes, and Abyssinians. The Siamese is a slender cat with blue eyes and a really loud meow. The Manx is a tailless breed. The Abyssinian looks like the cat that the ancient Egyptians worshipped.

Whether your cat is a purebred longhaired or shorthaired cat or a mixed-breed cat, it can make a good family pet.

Here are some questions you and your family may want to think about before you decide to get a pet cat.

- 🐾 Do you have enough room for a cat's food dish, water dish, and litter box?

- 🐾 Will your cat have to be indoors all the time or can it be allowed outdoors? Remember, all kinds of cats prey on birds. Consider putting a collar with a bell on your pet cat if you allow it to go outdoors.

- 🐾 Will you or other family members have the time and patience to care for a cat regularly?

- 🐾 Can your family make arrangements to take care of the cat if you go away for many days on a trip?

You also have to think about what kind of cat you want. Should you get a purebred or a mixed-breed cat? If you'd like a purebred cat, what kind do you want? Do you want a male or female cat? Do you want a kitten or an adult? Should you adopt a cat from an animal shelter or from a friend or buy one from a cat breeder? You and your family need to find out as much as you can about having a pet cat before making these decisions.

For many people, cats make ideal pets. Watching a cat is never dull. A cat loves to explore. It will play with a string or stalk an object. It will climb almost anything and get into the most unlikely places. It can be quiet or friendly with its owner. Cats are wonderful and mysterious animals. Just ask anyone who has ever owned a cat!

Using Mac OS X Lion Server

Charles Edge, Jr.

Beijing · Cambridge · Farnham · Köln · Sebastopol · Tokyo

Using Mac OS X Lion Server

by Charles Edge, Jr.

Published by O'Reilly Media, Inc., 1005 Gravenstein Highway North, Sebastopol, CA 95472.

O'Reilly books may be purchased for educational, business, or sales promotional use. Online editions are also available for most titles (*http://my.safaribooksonline.com*). For more information, contact our corporate/institutional sales department: (800) 998-9938 or *corporate@oreilly.com*.

Editor: Shawn Wallace	**Cover Designer:** Karen Montgomery
Production Editor: Kristen Borg	**Interior Designer:** David Futato
Proofreader: Jasmine Perez	**Illustrator:** Robert Romano

Revision History for the First Edition:

2012-03-15   First release

See *http://oreilly.com/catalog/errata.csp?isbn=9781449316051* for release details.

ISBN: 978-1-449-31605-1

[LSI]

1331753764

Table of Contents

Preface

People often ask me if I think Apple is a company that knows how to make a good server. My answer is usually a little longer than what those people probably had in mind. Tim Berners-Lee wrote the first web server in 1989 on a computer running the NeXTSTEP operating system. At the time, NeXTSTEP was a fledgling, Unix-like operating system that was in many ways a by-product of Steve Jobs leaving Apple in 1985. When Steve Jobs returned to Apple, he brought the Unix-like operating system (then known as OpenStep) with him. Over the course of the following decade, NeXTSTEP replaced the Apple operating system, ultimately becoming Mac OS X and Mac OS X Server.

The operating system that has evolved into Mac OS X hosted the first web server, but much has changed since 1989. Sure, Mac OS X Server still has a web server, although now it runs Apache. And Apache is one of the hundreds of open source products now built into Mac OS X Server. Mac OS X Server can now manage thousands of client computers using Open Directory and Profile Manager. Over the years, Mac OS X Server has been a file server, a podcasting server, a video streaming server, and an imaging server for Mac OS X client computers. Basically, Mac OS X Server can do most anything that administrators might want a server to do.

Mac OS X Server has now been Apple's server operating system for over 10 years. During this time, the server has undergone many changes. Out of the box, Mac OS X Server is an easy to use product that appeals to nontraditional server administrators. Once marketed as "open source made easy," the product has continued to get increasingly simple to use while still allowing for administrators to hack together their own solutions as Berners-Lee did in 1989.

However, the most substantial changes in the long history of Apple's server offering are in the latest version, Mac OS X Server 10.7, known as Lion Server. Mac OS X Server is just an app now. The app runs on Mac OS X, and installs some server-centric components during the initial setup. At the height of its server offerings, Apple had dedicated server hardware in the Apple Xserve and Xserve RAID, rack mountable dual power supply units that were "enterprise class" according to Apple. But hardware has gotten faster, and Apple has built a lot of iPads since the inception of the Xserve. Today,

Apple sells the Mac mini Server and the Mac Pro Server, both of which substantially out-perform the previous generations of hardware.

Given the perceived consumer class of hardware and the simplified user interface that Lion Server sports, many have labeled it as a home or small office operating system. The simple fact is that sure, Lion Server makes for a great server for homes and small offices. But Lion Server also scales and is more than capable as a utility server to manage Apple computers in large education environments, enterprises, and anywhere else you need a rocket ship of a computer.

Do I think that Apple makes good servers? Of course, otherwise I wouldn't be writing this book. But there is a huge caveat to that response: you have to buy into how Apple wants you to use a server. You have to be into the Mac mini form factor, a consumer-centric approach (which is explained throughout this book), or simply hacking together your own solutions using the many tools Apple bundles with the operating system, much like the founding fathers of the Internet did back in the waning days of the 1980s (although you don't have to listen to A Flock of Seagulls while doing so).

Audience

In many ways, the traditional system administrator will find Lion challenging in its consumeristic approach. There is a lot of power under the hood, but the tools used to manage the server have been simplified so that anyone can manage it, not just veteran Unix gods. The whole Apple experience is easy to manage in Lion, with an increasingly similar interface to iPads. Although managing a server isn't always going to be as easy as using an iPad, Apple is obviously leaning toward that direction with the basic tasks for Lion Server management. But Lion Server is a complex system, with many steps needing to be performed in a specific fashion in order to function properly.

My goal with this book is to show you how to manage a Lion Server. As such, beginning to intermediate system administrators will find this book a reference in getting started with an Apple server. Advanced Mac server system administrators will also find the book useful as a reference for quickly updating existing skills. But the book is really meant for new system administrators: the owner of the small business, the busy parent trying to manage all those iPhones and iPads the kids are running around with, the teacher with a classroom full of iMacs or iPads, and of course, the new podcaster, just looking for a place to host countless hours of talking about the topic of her choice. New Wave music, perhaps?

This book is not meant to be a definitive guide to Lion Server. I'd love to write one, but it's not what this book is. Seasoned system administrators may find certain aspects of the Lion interface challenging in how simplistic they are, and so will find value here. But this book doesn't cover managing a Lion Server from the command line, scripting client management, or other advanced topics.

Organization and Structure

One of the most important aspects of writing a book is to tell a cohesive story. However, technical books are often a bit more jumpy. Still, I have tried to establish a logical progression through the services covered. But as with most technical books, if you're looking to complete a specific task on a server, it may be a bit more like a *Choose Your Own Adventure* book.

The first two chapters of this book are about planning and installation. My recommendation is that you read Chapter 1 before you buy a server, Chapter 2 to help get it set up, and then the chapters that correspond to the services you will be running.

Chapter 1, *Planning*, covers various aspects of planning for a server installation. This includes choosing the correct hardware, and so is meant to be read before buying a computer to run Lion Server. This chapter also gives new administrators an idea of what goes into configuring the network to accommodate a server. More details for managing the network are mentioned in subsequent chapters, but the global aspects are covered here.

Chapter 2, *Installation*, provides a detailed look at installing Lion Server on a Mac OS X computer. This chapter does not cover upgrades, as Apple has done a good job of documenting the upgrade process on a per-server basis at support.apple.com (*http://www.apple.com/support/*). However, this chapter will prepare you for the various scenarios in Apple's support guides, coach you through correctly setting up the server on your first shot, and provide tips to keep at bay the gremlins that often necessitate a reinstallation.

In Chapter 3, *Sharing and Backing Up Files*, I discuss the most common service run on any server: sharing files. The chapter begins with managing the permissions to files, because if you cannot control access to data then it probably shouldn't be shared in the first place. Then I dive into a basic installation and look at connecting Windows, Mac, and iOS clients to the server. The chapter also covers backing up the server and clients using Apple's Time Machine and Time Machine Server.

Chapter 4, *Sharing Address Books, Calendars, and iChat*, covers groupware, or shared contacts, schedules, and instant messaging. I also cover configuring the Apple client applications to communicate with the server. Because managing a mail server now also involves mobile devices, contacts, calendars, and instant messaging, the mail component of modern groupware systems is handled in Chapter 6, *Building a Mail Server*.

Most installations of Mac OS X Server will likely end up running the web service at this point. Whether you need access to calendars, software updates, mail, podcasts, files for iOS devices or even client management resources (e.g., Profile Manager), these all require a functional web service. In Chapter 5, *Wikis, Webs, and Blogs*, I look at setting up the web service, as well as leveraging Apple's collaboration services: wikis and blogs.

Mail is one of the most under-appreciated services that are hosted by any server. Until mail goes down, that is. Much of the complexity of managing a mail server is in the ecosystem that is required to foster mail flowing to users (much of which is due to spammers). In Chapter 6, *Building a Mail Server*, I look at setting up the mail server. But more importantly, readers will be interested in the steps required to keep mail flowing and keep all of the various aspects of the systems surrounding the mail server healthy.

The iPod led to podcasts. Lion Server takes one of the hardest services to configure and makes it as simple as clicking an ON switch. Once set up though, there is a lot of work that goes into making your podcast available to anyone in the world. In Chapter 7, *Building Your Own Podcasting Server*, we'll look at those steps. And in no time, we'll have you explaining to the world why "Space Age Love Song" is your favorite song ever!

In Chapter 8, *Managing Apple Computers and iOS Devices*, we look at Managed Preferences and Profiles. Managed Preferences are the traditional method for managing the settings that get applied to Apple computers. Profiles are a new opt-in system from Apple that extends the concept of Managed Preferences to a Mobile Device Management (MDM) solution, capable of managing Lion and iOS-based devices alike.

Chapter 9, *Network Services*, helps initiate services for the rest of the network. This includes providing IP addresses to clients (DHCP), configuring name resolution so users don't have to keep track of the IP address of servers (DNS), using the server as a router, and Apple's favorite: VPNs. I also take a look at using Lion Server to manage AirPort base stations in the section on RADIUS.

Finally, Chapter 10, *Deploying Mac OS X Computers*, provides a guide to the mass deployment aspects built into Lion Server. These revolve around System Image Utility, NetRestore, NetInstall, and NetBoot.

Conventions Used in This Book

The following typographical conventions are used in this book:

Italic

> Indicates new terms, URLs, email addresses, filenames, and file extensions.

`Constant width`

> Used for program listings, as well as within paragraphs to refer to program elements such as variable or function names, databases, data types, environment variables, statements, and keywords.

`Constant width bold`

> Shows commands or other text that should be typed literally by the user.

`Constant width italic`

> Shows text that should be replaced with user-supplied values or by values determined by context.

This icon signifies a tip, suggestion, or general note.

 This icon indicates a warning or caution.

Using Code Examples

This book is here to help you get your job done. In general, you may use the code in this book in your programs and documentation. You do not need to contact us for permission unless you're reproducing a significant portion of the code. For example, writing a program that uses several chunks of code from this book does not require permission. Selling or distributing a CD-ROM of examples from O'Reilly books does require permission. Answering a question by citing this book and quoting example code does not require permission. Incorporating a significant amount of example code from this book into your product's documentation does require permission.

We appreciate, but do not require, attribution. An attribution usually includes the title, author, publisher, and ISBN. For example: "*Using Mac OS X Lion Server* by Charles Edge, Jr. (O'Reilly). Copyright 2012 Charles Edge, Jr., 978-1-449-31605-1."

If you feel your use of code examples falls outside fair use or the permission given above, feel free to contact us at *permissions@oreilly.com*.

Safari® Books Online

 Safari Books Online (*www.safaribooksonline.com*) is an on-demand digital library that delivers expert content in both book and video form from the world's leading authors in technology and business. Technology professionals, software developers, web designers, and business and creative professionals use Safari Books Online as their primary resource for research, problem solving, learning, and certification training.

Safari Books Online offers a range of product mixes and pricing programs for organizations, government agencies, and individuals. Subscribers have access to thousands of books, training videos, and prepublication manuscripts in one fully searchable database from publishers like O'Reilly Media, Prentice Hall Professional, Addison-Wesley Professional, Microsoft Press, Sams, Que, Peachpit Press, Focal Press, Cisco Press, John Wiley & Sons, Syngress, Morgan Kaufmann, IBM Redbooks, Packt, Adobe Press, FT Press, Apress, Manning, New Riders, McGraw-Hill, Jones & Bartlett, Course Technology, and dozens more. For more information about Safari Books Online, please visit us online.

How to Contact Us

Please address comments and questions concerning this book to the publisher:

O'Reilly Media, Inc.
1005 Gravenstein Highway North
Sebastopol, CA 95472
800-998-9938 (in the United States or Canada)
707-829-0515 (international or local)
707-829-0104 (fax)

We have a web page for this book, where we list errata, examples, and any additional information. You can access this page at:

http://shop.oreilly.com/product/0636920022664.do

To comment or ask technical questions about this book, send email to:

bookquestions@oreilly.com

For more information about our books, courses, conferences, and news, see our website at *http://www.oreilly.com*.

Find us on Facebook: *http://facebook.com/oreilly*

Follow us on Twitter: *http://twitter.com/oreillymedia*

Watch us on YouTube: *http://www.youtube.com/oreillymedia*

Acknowledgements

Shawn Wallace at O'Reilly was a huge help in guiding me through the O'Reilly way of publishing. He was also instrumental in defining the tone of the book and helped along the way (especially with all those screen shots we were able to dump). Marsee Henon has also been a huge help over the years with various user groups that I'm connected with and keeping me supplied with a flow of O'Reilly books that helped me learn how to do much of the open source side of the Mac Server. And a special thanks goes out to Brian Jepson for helping get this thing kicked off! Thanks also to the more than 100 O'Reilly authors whose animal books sit on my shelves at home. The home decorating is so much easier with that rainbow of book jackets!

The Mac system administration community is by far the best IT community in the world. I stand on their shoulders. No single person could learn how to manage all the components of a Mac OS X Server (especially from the command line) on their own without at least some assistance from the community. From Macworld (now MacIT) to MacTech to MacSysAdmin, there are hundreds of talented engineers and technical writers who have shaped our community into one that embraces an open transfer of knowledge and helping others. I am lucky to count you all among my friends and look forward to many more years on Twitter, hanging out at camps and at Dave's.

Big thanks to Arek Dreyer and Ben Greisler for their continued work and support of the Apple Pro Training Series, as well as all the people who contributed to Server Essentials and provided guidance, in whatever form, to the community.

Also I'd like to thank the good people at Apple. The products that Apple makes are why my career (and this book) is possible. The quality with which Lion Server has been crafted is a testament to all that Apple stands for. Those at Apple Training, Apple Enterprise, and Apple Education: thanks for being the conduit for the Mac admin community, for listening to all the good and bad things we have to say, and for being our voice within Apple.

Finally, this book is dedicated to my wife and daughter. It is time taken from you that allows me to keep writing these books. Thanks for the love and encouragement.

CHAPTER 1

Planning

As with all technical things, measure twice, cut once. But how much time to spend measuring depends in large part on how complicated your environment is. There are a lot of factors that go into planning a server appropriately, such as heating and cooling, the physical machine that will be the server, and even how the server will be backed up.

You can spend an unlimited amount of money on a server. Or you can spend next to nothing and buy a used Mac mini on eBay. The scale of your purchase and the complexity of the deployment are two very independent concepts though. In this chapter, we're going to look at, well, basically what you should buy before you get started installing that spiffy server of yours (and, importantly, whether you should buy something different than the shiny box you already have in your hands).

The Minimum

By default, Lion Server is installed from the Mac App Store on a computer that is already running Mac OS X Lion. The minimum requirements for the computer that you install Lion Server on will be the following:

- 64-bit Intel processor
- 2 gigabytes of RAM
- 10 gigabytes of available hard drive space
- Access to the Mac App Store on the Internet

These settings are the minimum requirements for Lion Server, but most servers require far more resources. Resources such as hard drive space, memory, and even items that aren't part of the server itself but are part of the ecosystem that acts to supplement it are important to plan for in advance. For example, if there isn't any Internet access on the server before you sit down to install it, then you might need to take the server to a place that does have Internet access or plan on imaging the server using a traditional imaging solution before wasting time on what would be a failed installation.

Server Allocation

One of the first factors to decide is how many servers you need. For most OS X Server environments, the answer is going to be one. But the impact that scale has on the rest of the options we cover throughout this chapter cannot be discounted.

For an environment with 5 to 10 users, as would be common with a typical home environment, any of the hardware mentioned previously will suffice whatever your needs may be, with one exception: hard drive space. We'll discuss drive capacities later in this chapter, but for now we can consider a few indicators that you need to consider a second server (or more):

- **You have 300 or more users:** One Mac Pro can typically run things like portable home directories for a good 300 users simultaneously.
- **System resources are getting crushed:** Looking at the Activity Monitor shows overly high utilization in at least one category, although frequently in more than one.
- **Business stops when a server goes offline:** Organizations can be severely impacted when a server goes offline. Most notably, if a web server cannot accept customer orders or a mail server is not available.

Although some general rules can be helpful, nothing is more useful in determining utilization statistics and planning for future purchases than monitoring software. There are a lot of monitoring software packages, including Lithium (*http://www.lithium5 .com*), Dartware's Intermapper (*http://www.intermapper.com*), and Nagios (*http://www .nagios.org*), all of which have specific tools for monitoring Mac OS X Servers.

Service Allocation

No matter how many servers you elect to use, the next question to answer is what services to run. Anytime you get a shiny new piece of technology, it is tempting to enable everything that can be done with it. However, doing so with Lion Server will produce a server that runs more slowly than it should. Instead, plan ahead and know which services to enable before unboxing the product, and more specifically, which services to enable on each server.

Lion Server runs in a multimaster configuration. The directory services (explained more in Chapter 2) are effectively a master on each server. This means that any server that is a directory server acts as a master that replicates with the Open Directory Master.

Choosing the Right Hardware

Most traditional server administrators (including OS X Server administrators) would consider a server running on a Mac mini, iMac, or even a laptop to be silly. But things are changing at a rapid pace, and that which once seemed silly can easily seem like a really good idea. For example, if you have a cart of 40 iPads and you need a server to manage them, then you aren't likely to find a better combo punch than running Lion Server on a MacBook Air.

But if you are performing computationally complex calculations to render video (as is common with large Podcast Producer environments), then you will more than likely need far more firepower than a workstation with 2 gigs of RAM can net.

The choices you have in front of you for hardware:

Mac Pro
> Usually the best solution if you can afford it. Apple's desktop system that comes with plenty of drive bays for hard drives, a RAID card that can be added (which we'll cover in "Storage" on page 3), two Ethernet ports, optional fibre channel, and a Wi-Fi port.

iMac
> Apple's desktop computer with a built-in video screen. Likely only suitable for systems that run a shared workstation that is also a server.

Mac mini
> Apple's most popular server product, a miniature computer that is actually faster than the last version of the Xserve.

MacBook Air
> Apple's entry-level laptop offering that comes with solid state drives (making it great to sit atop big old carts of mobile systems).

MacBook Pro
> Apple's high-end portable computer offering. Still great on top of a cart, but should probably have its lid closed before moving the cart (not that I'm advocating leaving the lid of a MacBook Air open while pushing a cart around a busy school).

Apple once had a rack mount server called the Xserve for those requiring rack density, but no longer sells that product. It is still possible to put any Apple hardware on rack shelves (although a big old iMac might look awkward in a 19-inch rack). The Mac mini is likely one of the more attractive systems to run in a rack, as two can be installed side by side in a standard rack mount enclosure.

Storage

Storage is one of the easier items to discuss. But one of the harder items to plan for capacity on, due to the rapid explosion of file sizes and of disk sizes for that matter, is disk utilization. The best way to do this is again with monitoring. By looking at the average increase in storage consumption, you can get a good projection on how much data you will need over time.

One thing everyone with the option should look at is leveraging a RAID to keep data protected. RAIDs are not for backup, but more to keep from having to restore a backup.

There are a few different types of RAIDs, which are referred to as RAID levels. These include:

RAID 0

No redundancy, the total capacity is the added storage of all drives that are members of the RAID set. Only use this when you don't mind losing a disk. The tradeoff is usually faster media.

RAID 1

Full mirror, total capacity is half of a two drive RAID set. Typically used in Mac mini Servers with two drives and with Mac Pro Servers with two drives.

RAID 3

RAID with one parity drive, total capacity is roughly 2/3 to 4/5 of the total amount of data. If any drive is lost, then it is rebuilt with the static parity drive. Not frequently used on a Mac due to RAID 5 and RAID 6 preference.

RAID 5

RAID with one parity drive that is split across a slice of every disk in the raid set. Probably the most common in OS X environments (minimum of three drives).

RAID 6

Same as RAID 5, but with two parity drives. Maximum level of data security in a Mac OS X environment (usually found on Promise hardware, not natively in Apple computers given the number of drives, etc.).

Lower-tiered storage is pretty cheap though. Don't feel like you need to spend a lot of money today. Buying storage is a lot like buying a car: the second you drive the storage out of the parking lot, it isn't worth anything (mostly because a drive twice the size is probably going to be out within 24 months). This isn't to say that there aren't smart ways to spend on storage. For example, if you are only going to spend an extra $100 on a server to get 3TB drives over 2TB drives, then that's probably worth the spend.

System Resources

As referenced in "Choosing the Right Hardware" on page 2, when the system resources for a single server environment exceeds the acceptable threshold for what a single server can do, you will need two or more servers. But how much of a load can one system take before it gets saturated and needs either an upgrade or replacement? Well, that is a tough nut to crack, given that everyone's data is different: different sizes, different file types, different compression types, different types of network equipment, and even different clients. This makes estimating the exact impact of services pretty difficult.

Apple does not publish information indicating how many servers you need or how many users per server. However, Apple does test each Mac mini Server with up to 36 users using typical home directories. Although you can use far more than 36 users on a mini, the number is dependent on the types of files and how intensely each file type in use interacts with the server. For example, if you aren't using centralized home directories and instead you are just using iCal Server, you can likely have hundreds of users connect to a single mini. A Mac Pro Server, on the other hand, can often sustain hundreds of users connecting to file shares and interacting with the server regularly with portable or mobile home directories.

Given that most who purchase a server will have access to someone that can assist with appropriate sizing, that is a good place to look for assistance with this conundrum. One option is to work with Apple directly. When purchasing a server, an Apple reseller can guide you through picking the right hardware. Also, members of the Apple Consultants Network (*http://consultants.apple.com*) can assist if your reseller cannot.

Backup

You can spend less than $100 per year to back up your servers, you can buy a Time Machine for a onetime cost of a few hundred dollars, or you can buy a tape library, establish an offsite rotation of the tapes and acquire one of the various software packages to back up your systems. Some options for available software packages include the following:

Time Machine
> Time Machine is the tool that Apple includes with Lion (and Lion Server). Time Machine can back up to hard drives, Apple Time Capsules, disks attached to Air-Port base stations, and over smoke signals (OK, so not so much on the smoke signals, but it would be pretty cool if it could, right?).

CrashPlan
> The cloud is the next best thing to smoke signals. CrashPlan is a really intelligently designed solution that deduplicates data (meaning it backs up parts of files rather than complete files each time you make a change to the data) and then backs up the data either to the CrashPlan cloud or to your own disks.

Retrospect
> Retrospect is one of the oldest and most mature of Apple solutions. Retrospect can back up to disk and tape.

PresSTORE
> PresSTORE is another tool that can back up to disk and tape, with a great system used to back multiple clients up.

Bakbone and Atempo
> Two similar products, built for backing up even more data on a larger scale, commonly in cross-platform environments that need specialized agents for Windows and other platforms.

Symantec's Backup Exec and Tivoli Storage Manager
> Similar to any number of other Windows-based backup solutions that are Windows-centric but have agents available for Mac OS X and other platforms.

There is much more information on leveraging Time Machine for backing up Lion client computers and Lion servers in Chapter 3.

One of the best parts of choosing software is that you can often get software developers to help you choose hardware that is compatible with their products. If you are backing up to disk, then there is an almost universal compatibility between products. However, if backing up to tape, then you might want to check with the various tape developers to see if there are supported drivers for a given platform.

Once you know what kind of backup storage, then look at how much data changes on a given system each day. The average of this is what you refer to as the rate of change. A full backup of data plus the amount of data per each day whose history you want to store is the amount that each backup set should have in it. For example, if you want seven days of backup and a full backup set is 10 terabytes with a 500 gigabyte rate of change per day, then you would calculate 10TB+(500GB*7) for a total of 13.5 terabytes of data. If you want to always keep one of these sets offsite (and you should in most cases), then that would double the total to 27 terabytes.

Overall, these same general formulas are typically applicable no matter the software title or hardware used. Those 27 terabytes can be disk, tape, or carrier pigeon provided you have the right combination of tools. This even extends to having part of the data in tape and another part in disk. For example, in order to allow for more rapid data restoration, it's common to do the daily differential backups to disk and the fulls to tape.

Power

Every server should be on an uninterruptable power supply (UPS). The Mac mini Server has very low power requirements. As such, it usually isn't going to need to have the kind of UPS that powers small cities. But...then again, if you have 500 Xserves, consider something more than an entry-level product from Best Buy.

Let's start with some numbers:

- The Mac mini runs between 10 watts (idle) and 85 watts (maximum) per hour
- The Mac Pro runs between 115 watts (idle) and 263 watts (maximum) per hour
- The iMac runs between 94 watts (idle) and 241 watts (maximum) per hour
- The 11-inch MacBook Air runs at approximately 35 watts per hour (or 50 for the 13-inch)
- The MacBook Pro runs between 15 (idle) and 65 (maximum) watts per hour

The UPS devices should run on either USB or a network connection that has client software available for Lion. This is basically included in every UPS built in the past 10 years, so given that the shelf life of most UPSes is lower than most systems that can currently run Lion Server, chances are you'll use a UPS with support for automated shutdown.

 Although it is arguable that MacBook Air and MacBook Pro computers have built-in batteries and do not need battery backup in a UPS, it is still critical to make sure they have ample surge protection.

Planning Your Server's Network Configuration

One of the most important things to do on any computer is to configure the network settings properly. On a server, this is even more important than on client computers, which often pull their network connections dynamically, making them somewhat of a zero configuration affair. On a server, the settings need to be static, and so before you start installing the server, you need to define them.

Mac OS X 10.6 and below had a different operating system for the server product than for the client product. The installer was different, you booted to optical media or an image to run the installation, and during the setup process for the server, you had to type in the IP address and other network information. In Lion Server, you run Lion before installing Lion Server. Therefore, this information has presumably been provided as part of the OS X configuration.

But you should still configure these items before installing the Lion Server software from the App Store. The first step is to obtain the IP address, subnet mask, and gateway settings before you install anything.

Determining the IP Address, Subnet Mask, and Gateway

The various network settings installed on a server come from the network environment. If you have an AirPort, Linksys, or other device guarding your network and splitting your IP address so others can use it, then you likely have full control over what settings you use on the network. If you are installing OS X Server into a much larger environment, then you likely do not have control and need to obtain the correct settings to use from a network administrator.

Configuring DHCP

If you have control over the network devices, then the most important aspect of choosing an IP address is that it is not in the DHCP pool. DHCP, or Dynamic Host Control Protocol, is how computers receive IP addresses automatically when they are configured to do so. In smaller networks, the DHCP pool is often defined and IP addresses allocated by the router. There are a number of options for routers, but we'll just look at the Apple AirPort in this example. However, the concepts apply to any router you may be using.

To look at the DHCP settings on an Apple AirPort, first open AirPort Utility from /
Applications/Utilities. Then click on Manual Setup and then on the Internet button in
the AirPort Utility toolbar. Next, click on the Internet Connection tab and verify that
the Connection Sharing field is set to "Share a public IP address," as shown in Figure 1-1. This means that DHCP is automatically enabled.

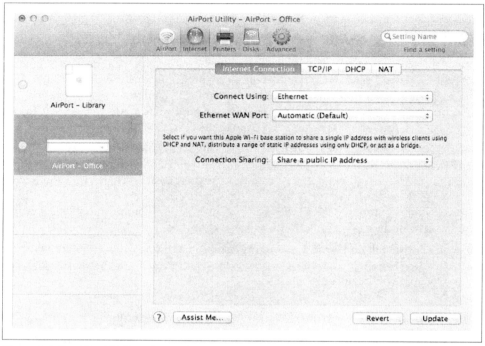

Figure 1-1. Enabling NAT on the Apple AirPort

To then see the DHCP settings, click on the DHCP tab. Here, the beginning and ending
IP addresses are defined. The IP address you choose for your server should not be one
of these. IP addresses range from .1 on the network to .254. Given that the gateway, or
router, is typically one of these, the server is often best set to .2 through .253. For
example, if your gateway is 192.168.210.1, then the server can easily be set to
192.168.210.2. You would then change the DHCP Beginning Address from
192.168.210.2 to 192.168.210.3 (as in Figure 1-2) so that the scope of your DHCP
addresses does not include the IP address you are using for the server. Keeping the IP
address low in this fashion helps you to remember which IP address the server is using,
although for the most part the goal will be to access the server by a name (e.g.,
home.krypted.com) rather than accessing the server by an IP address.

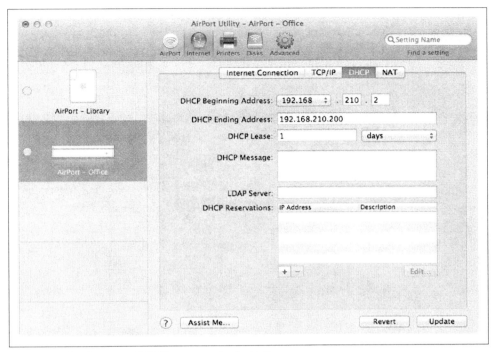

Figure 1-2. Configuring a DHCP scope on Apple AirPort

The IP address is a unique address used to access the server and should not be used by any other devices on that network. The subnet mask, gateway, and DNS servers will also need to be configured in order to access the server, have it route traffic to the Internet, and access other computers by name (respectively).

Finding the Subnet Mask and Gateway

The subnet mask defines the size of the network. By default, the subnet mask is configured as 255.255.255.0 on an Apple AirPort and most other consumer-level routers. The setting that is used on an Apple AirPort can be found by opening AirPort Utility from */Applications/Utilities* and clicking on the Internet button in the AirPort Utility toolbar. From here, click on the TCP/IP tab and the Subnet Mask field will show the setting that you will most likely use on the server (whether the server is wired or runs wirelessly).

The IP address and subnet mask is required to configure TCP/IP in Mac OS X. Although most environments will still use a gateway and DNS settings, they are not required. The IP address and subnet mask have been fairly straightforward to determine thus far. The gateway can be a slightly more complicated affair because the wireless access point can act as the gateway, but isn't always. If the AirPort is the gateway, then you can use the IP address from Figure 1-3. Otherwise, you will most likely use the gateway that is listed in AirPort Utility. A router, which in this context is synonymous with a gateway, connects two networks.

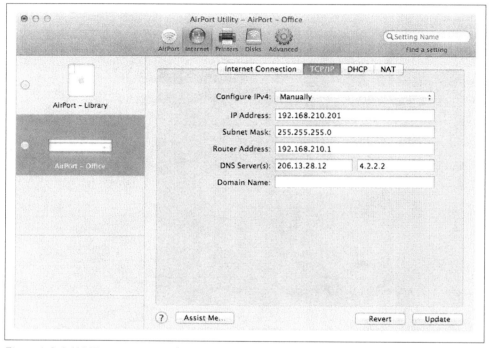

Figure 1-3. LAN IP settings on Apple AirPort

A router can also translate a single IP address into a network using Network Address Translation, a protocol used for placing a number of devices behind a single IP. This IP would often be a routable IP address, or one that can be used to access resources from outside the network. Isolating an improperly configured gateway setting is a straightforward affair. If you can connect client computers to the server from inside the network but cannot connect remotely (and can access other computers internally but not access external resources), then you more than likely have an improperly configured gateway setting. This test pertains to IP address-based communications only.

What's In a Name?: DNS

Accessing resources by name rather than IP address is controlled by DNS, or Domain Name System. Lion Server can run a DNS server of its own, allowing it to cache and serve naming information for client computers (one of the client computers often being itself). When you provide a name server to OS X, you can use other DNS servers in your organization, DNS servers provided by your Internet service provider (i.e., your DSL or cable provider) or itself.

Before you install the Server app on a Lion computer, verify that the computer's name matches what the DNS server has configured for the IP address the server will live on. In order to do so, use the Ping tab in Network Utility (located at */Applications/Utilities*) to try to access the name of the host. When open, provide the name in the "Enter the network address to ping" field and then click on the Ping button. The server will then attempt to resolve the hostname. If it can resolve the name, then the IP address that the server responded with will be listed in the output, similar to that in Figure 1-4.

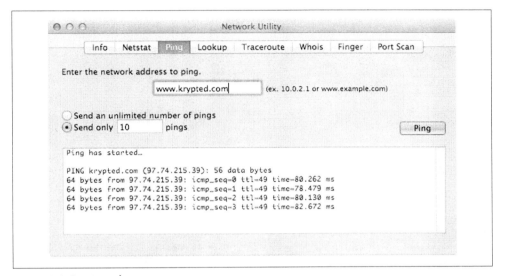

Figure 1-4. Pinging a hostname

 If the ping fails, do not be alarmed, as you may not have configured the server yet.

Servers should be accessible by name and IP address. In DNS, a PTR record is used to associate a default name that IP addresses respond to. If clients point to a DNS server you control, then you can configure both on your DNS server.

Testing that the name appropriately responds with the IP address is important. But equally as important for many environments is configuring the reverse IP address as well. To check that the IP address has the appropriate name configured, open Network Utility and then click on the Lookup tab. Enter the address of the server and then click on the Lookup button. Provided that the response contains the hostname of the server, then your servers are configured appropriately, as in Figure 1-5.

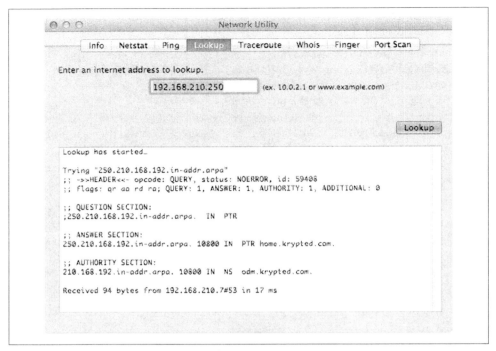

Figure 1-5. Network utility and PTR records

When installing OS X Server, the server will check that the DNS configuration matches the hostnames and IP address(es) on the server. If they do not, then the DNS service will be installed automatically and any issues will be remedied on the local DNS service. These DNS settings would then only be applicable for client computers with the DNS server running on the Lion Server applied. We will cover DNS further in Chapter 2.

Link Aggregation

Link aggregation bonds two or more network ports so that they act as one. This provides failover and increased throughput. If a cable or a port is severed, connections to servers still function. The bandwidth of multiple ports is also aggregated, giving twice the throughput or more.

Before configuring link aggregation, it will need to be set up on the switch. Each brand of switch has a different process for setting this up. Link aggregation configuration on switches is a complex and advanced topic typically handled by network administrators, and so we will not cover that portion of link aggregation.

To configure link aggregation from within Lion, open the Network System Preference pane and click on the icon of a cogwheel and then click on the option to Manage Virtual Interfaces. From the Manage Virtual Interfaces screen, click on the plus sign ("+") and then click on the New Link Aggregate… option. Provide a name for the link aggregated network and then check the box for each interface to include in the aggregated port, as in Figure 1-6.

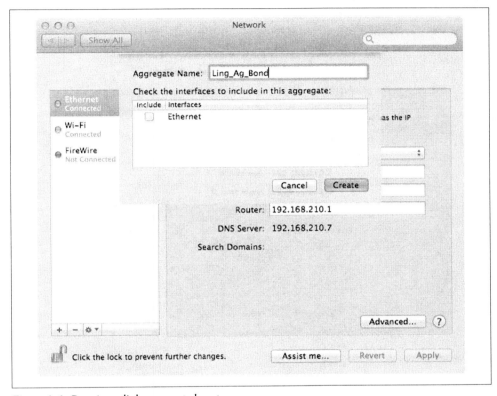

Figure 1-6. Creating a link aggregated port

When you are happy with the configuration of the ports in the bond, click on Create to complete the bonds configuration. The port configuration will then be green, provided the bond is functioning.

 The Xserve has two interfaces. Either can be used for Lights Out Management, a feature that allows administrators to reboot systems remotely. However, if you use Link Aggregation on the two ports, Lights Out Management will no longer function on the server.

Using Multiple IP Addresses

Servers are capable of using multiple IP addresses. Mac Pro and Xserve computers have two network interfaces installed. Apple also sells network interfaces, as do a number of third-party entities. Additionally, each interface can run multiple IP addresses, providing a practically infinite number of options for interfaces and addresses.

Using multiple IP addresses on a single port is known as multihoming. In order to configure a single interface to have two IP addresses, use the plus sign ("+") to bring up the "Select the interface and enter a name for the new service" screen. Here, select the network interface you would like to configure a second IP for and provide a name for the second instance of the interface (Figure 1-7).

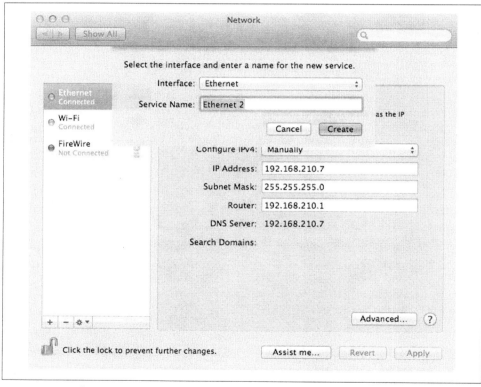

Figure 1-7. Configuring multiple hardware ports

Click on Create and the second port will be listed in the Network System Preference pane. The port can then be configured as any other port would be.

Accessing the Server from Outside the Network

Once you get your addresses appropriately configured, many will want to access their server from outside of their local networks. There are a few different strategies to provide external access. One is to configure access for anyone using the WAN IP address for your environment. The other is to configure access for any clients using a given iCloud account, which requires little to no further configuration. Given that the first is the most common (for now), let's start there.

Port Forwarding

Each network service uses one or more TCP/IP ports to receive a connection from the outside world. The most common combination is port 80 being used for web connections. TCP/IP uses ports to direct traffic for a given IP address to the appropriate service.

The popular site on OS X Server and system administration, afp548.com (*http://afp548.com*), owes its name to the fact that 548 is the port number used to access AFP, the default file sharing service for Mac OS X computers to talk to one another.

One of the coolest features of OS X Server is the ability to automatically configure an Apple AirPort, provided that the AirPort is being used as a router, to forward ports for services enabled on the server. Provided you are using an Apple AirPort as a router, you need only give the server the password to manage the router and it will do all the work for you.

The manual for every router on the market also explains how to configure port forwarding. Given the variety of routers on the market, further explanation of port forwards per device is best then left to said manuals.

Accessing the Server Using DNS

Earlier in this chapter, we looked at configuring the server to be able to access other resources by name. When you are outside of the network, you likely don't want to have to remember some long string of numbers just to access the server. Therefore, most will want to configure some kind of a name to access their server. There are a couple of ways to go about doing so in a smaller environment. The first is statically, or configuring a domain that you own to point at a server while the second is using dynamic DNS, to update a third-party DNS service that is easily configured (although it may require an additional cost).

Configuring DNS

The first option is to configure DNS for a domain or name that you own. To do so, you must first have what is known as Start of Authority (SOA) for the domain. For larger environments, contacting a DNS administrator is typically required to perform such a DNS configuration. But in a smaller environment, if you own the domain name, you can do pretty much anything (within technical reason of course) that you like.

To look up the owner of a domain, we will again turn to the Network Utility, located in */Applications/Utilities*. From Network Utility, click on the Whois button and enter the domain name (e.g., krypted.com) into the "Enter a domain address to look up its 'whois' information" field.

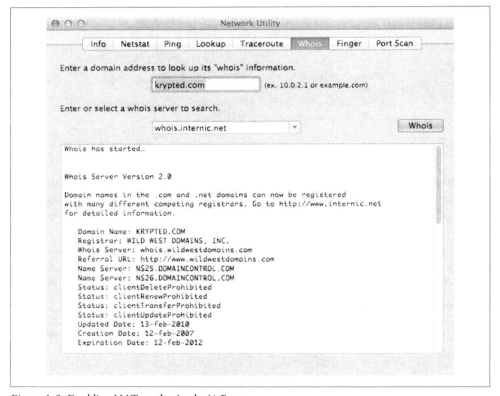

Figure 1-8. Enabling NAT on the Apple AirPort

The address of the DNS servers and the name of the registrar is displayed in the output, as you can see in Figure 1-8. The registrar is where the domain was purchased and therefore who controls settings for the domain. Most registrars (all that I am aware of at least) provide a web control panel to configure DNS servers, and if you are using their DNS servers, also provide the ability to control DNS without the use of third-party DNS servers. If you log into your account with the registrar, then you should be able to configure a name for access into your network.

 This type of configuration will work for most services, with the exception of mail. For more on configuring DNS for mail services, see Chapter 9, where configuring mail servers is configured.

Setting up Dynamic DNS

Dynamic DNS is a third-party option provided by a number of companies. Dynamic DNS updates a DNS entry every time your server reboots. This is often used by people who don't have a domain name, or in environments where a static IP address cannot be obtained. The dynamic DNS servers are updated each time the server or router gets a new IP address.

Dynamic DNS is a great little tool for some environments. For larger production environments, it can represent another moving part that can break, but for smaller environments, where mission critical access is not required for the services installed on the server, dynamic DNS is perfectly acceptable.

The dynamic DNS service uses an agent running on your network to update the IP address it has on file for your environment. Many routers support using dynamic DNS. Most dynamic DNS services also have clients for Mac OS X. One such is DynDNS, which has a free client available at *http://dyn.com/dns/dyndns-free*. The first step to setting up dynamic DNS using such a service is to create an account with the company that provides the service. Doing so is different for each service, so we won't look at the specifics in doing so.

Once the account is created, most services will have an application that runs on the client computers to update the dynamic DNS service. DynDNS, one of the more popular services, has a client called DynDNS Updater (Figure 1-9). Open the Updater application and log in with the username and password that was created at the site. Once authenticated, click on the "Site" in the DynDNS Updater sidebar. Then, check the "Enable updating for this host" box and provide the hostname defined in the DynDNS web portal in the "Host name" field. Finally, choose the network interface that you wish the site to use (e.g., if you have multiple network interfaces).

Once the settings are configured as needed, check that the IP address updates on the website when the address changes. If it does, then you are able to access your servers by name using the DynDNS name selected for the hostname.

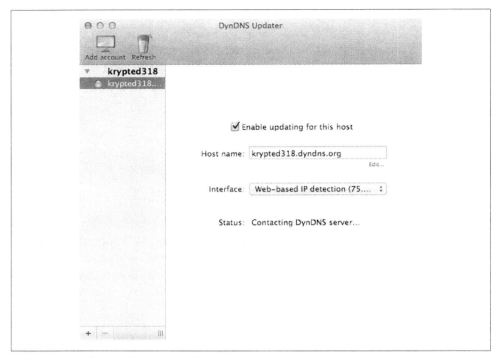

Figure 1-9. Configuring dynamic DNS

Configuring iCloud for Back to My Mac

As mentioned earlier, a network can be accessible using iCloud. iCloud requires your router be configured to allow UPnP networking. Most routers ship with this option enabled by default, as it is needed for most gaming consoles and other productive uses of time. Provided that UPnP is enabled, iCloud establishes a tunnel between your two computers through Apple, given that both are constantly in touch with the Apple servers.

Configuring computers to be accessible via iCloud isn't necessarily about providing web services to anyone in the world. It's more about configuring your computers to be able to access each other (and only each other) for sharing files, accessing the desktops of one another, and sharing contacts, calendars, and bookmarks. If this is what you want, then open the iCloud System Preference pane from System Preferences. Here, enter your iCloud information or click on the Create Account button to set up a new iCloud account for free.

When an account is associated with iCloud, a number of checkboxes will appear, as can be seen in Figure 1-10. Locate the option for Back to My Mac and check the box to enable the service.

Figure 1-10. Enabling Back to My Mac

Once checked, all computers using the same iCloud account will have access to one another via the Finder's Sidebar. To access the system, open a Finder screen and you will see them listed in the list of shared devices, as seen in Figure 1-11.

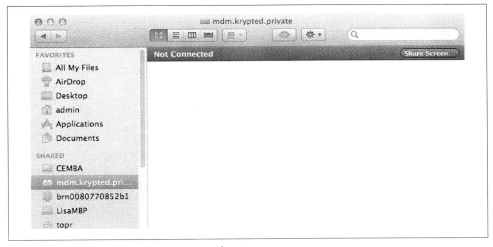

Figure 1-11. Accessing a Back to My Mac Client

Conclusion

A single Mac OS X Server configuration is usually pretty straightforward. But there are a lot of factors that go into planning such a deployment, even on a Mac mini running Lion Server. Storage, system resources, backup, power, backup, service allocation, backup, and Apple hardware are all important things to consider (did I mention backup?). They all comprise the ecosystem that the server lives in.

In this chapter, we looked at a number of things that everyone should consider. But planning networks and servers is a bit of a complicated task, and so there's no way we can ever dive into all of it. This chapter looks at most of the common things to do before you buy your server or before you start installing that mini server you just brought home. Once you're pretty satisfied with your server planning, it's time to move on to Chapter 2 and get to the installation process!

Installation

Installing Mac OS X Lion Server can take a little while, based on your bandwidth. This is because you have to download and install Mac OS X Lion and then download and install Mac OS X Lion Server. Each can be a substantial download.

If you are installing a lot of systems, then you can use the techniques described in Chapter 10, where you use a local installer that you custom build for the purpose of installing multiple systems at once.

Base OS Installation

Installing Lion is one of the easiest things to do in Lion Server. It's also the first thing you have to do. The best technique I can provide is for a clean installation, or a fresh installation on a new system. However, this doesn't necessarily work very well for people with servers running operating systems previous to Lion (e.g., Snow Leopard) that would like to upgrade. For those systems, see the Lion Server: Upgrading and Migrating guide (*http://images.apple.com/macosx/server/docs/Upgrading_and_Migrating_v10.7 .pdf*).

Making a Lion Recovery Disk

The first step to installing Lion for many is to create a Lion Recovery Disk. The Lion Recovery Disk is created using the Lion Recovery Disk Assistant, freely available at *http://support.apple.com/kb/DL1433*. When run, the Lion Recovery Disk Assistant takes a USB drive and turns it into a disk that can be used to install Lion over the Internet.

Once the Recovery Disk Assistant has been downloaded, open it and agree to the licensing agreement. Then the Recovery Disk Assistant will show all disks capable of being turned into a bootable installation drive. Click on a USB drive with at least 1 gigabyte of free space and then click on the Continue button (Figure 2-1).

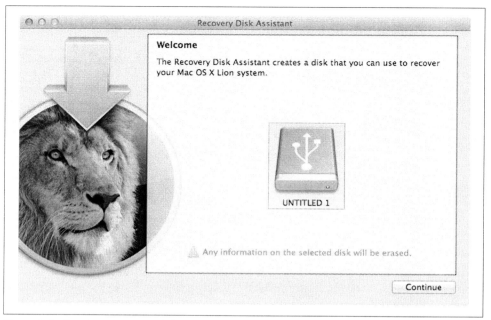

Figure 2-1. Creating a recovery disk

The assistant then creates the boot disk. To boot to the disk, boot an Apple computer while holding down the Option key and select the drive called Recovery HD.

When booted from the recovery drive, if there is an Ethernet connection that has a valid DHCP server to dynamically assign IP addresses, the client computer should be able to access the Internet. If not, and you need to use a wireless network for installation, use the AirPort menu in the upper-right corner of the screen to select a wireless network. At the Mac OS X Utilities screen, you should then be able to install OS X by clicking on the Reinstall Mac OS X option and then clicking on the Continue button (Figure 2-2).

At the Install Mac OS X screen, click on Continue. The computer's eligibility will then be checked, and if Lion needs to be purchased you can do so at this time. Otherwise, click Agree to accept Apple's licensing agreement, select the volume to install Lion onto, and then click on Install.

The installer will then install the computer, reboot, and you can proceed with registering the computer and configuring various settings, such as the IP address, hostname, and other settings, which are covered in the next few sections.

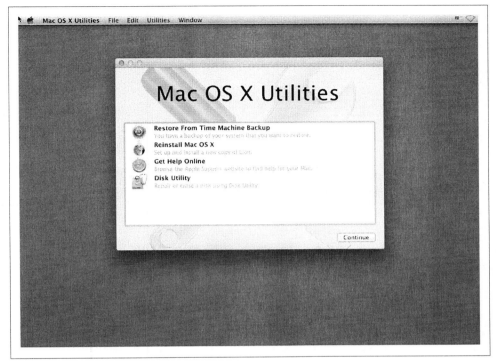

Figure 2-2. Installing Mac OS X Lion

Configuring the Network

Chapter 1 stepped you through determining the network settings to use on your OS X Server. At this point, you should have a static IP address and a subnet mask. You should probably also have a gateway, DNS servers, a properly configured DNS entry for the name you will be using on your server, and a properly configured PTR record for the IP address you will be using on the server.

In order to configure the TCP/IP settings, open the Network System Preference pane from System Preferences. Here, click on the adapter that will be the main network interface and click on the Using DHCP option in the Configure IPv4 field and select Manually. Then complete the following fields (Figure 2-3):

IP Address
> The IP address on the local network (LAN) that other users of that network use to access the server

Subnet Mask
> The subnet mask for the local network (LAN) that all users of that network use to access other devices on the network

Gateway
   The router for the network

DNS Server (under the Advanced button)
   The name servers for the environment (or 127.0.0.1 if the server is to be the DNS
   server)

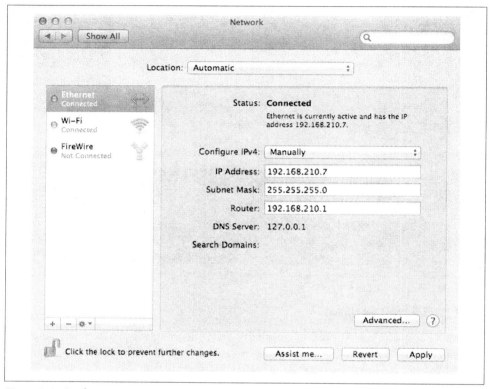

Figure 2-3. Configuring TCP/IP in Mac OS X

Once you have configured the TCP/IP information, click on the Apply button. The
server should then be able to access the Internet (provided the Internet is accessible on
the network).

Verifying Hostnames

Next, verify that the hostname of the server matches what you configured in DNS. This
can most easily be done using the hostname command. Running this command from
the Terminal application (available in the */Applications/Utilities* directory) will show
you the name of the server:

    hostname

If the output of the hostname command is not what you expect (or desire), then use the scutil command to check the name of the computer as well. This one is a little longer, but provides verification of the hostname:

```
sudo scutil -get HostName
```

 When running commands prefixed with sudo, you will be asked to enter your password. If the escalation of your privileges to run the command fails, then try running it again when logged in as an administrative user.

If the name still does not match the anticipated output, then you will need to set the name manually. To do so, run:

```
sudo scutil -set HostName
```

DNS translates the computer's name to an IP address. The hostname that you have should then be referenced against the DNS settings for your environment. Running the dig command followed by the hostname will tell you the IP address that the hostname points to:

```
dig www.krypted.com
```

Responds with:

```
; <<>> DiG 9.7.3-P3 <<>> www.krypted.com
;; global options: +cmd
;; Got answer:
;; ->>HEADER<<- opcode: QUERY, status: NOERROR, id: 60893
;; flags: qr rd ra; QUERY: 1, ANSWER: 2, AUTHORITY: 0, ADDITIONAL: 0

;; QUESTION SECTION:
;www.krypted.com.            IN      A

;; ANSWER SECTION:
>www.krypted.com.    3600   IN      CNAME   krypted.com.
krypted.com.         3600   IN      A       97.74.215.39
```

IP addresses also have hostnames assigned to them. Running dig against the IP address requires adding the ptr option and then taking the IP address, turning it around, and running dig against it followed by .in-addr.arpa. The ptr option comes from the fact that you are checking the IP addresses ptr, or pointer record, most commonly used for providing a name that should be associated with IP addresses. This may seem complicated, but in the following example, note that we are taking our IP address (in this case, 192.168.210.10) and running the command using it in reverse, with the .in-addr.arpa at the end:

```
dig ptr 10.210.168.192.in-addr.arpa
```

If the output does not have a name in the ANSWER SECTION (or more likely does not have an ANSWER SECTION if the ptr record for the IP address is misconfigured), then contact the administrator who has control over the DNS of your environment. If there are no DNS servers in the environment and the OS X Server will be the DNS server, then go ahead and proceed with installation and upon completion, the server will be running a DNS server with the correcting records.

Configuring Energy Saver

By default, OS X computers put themselves to sleep automatically. This is good on client computers, but bad on servers, which should always be accessible. Therefore, an important step to setting up an OS X Server is to tell the server not to go to sleep, so that you will still be able to share files, manage iOS devices, and access that shopping list whenever you need it.

Manage energy settings by clicking on the System Preferences under the Apple menu and clicking on the Energy Saver System Preference pane. The slider for "Computer sleep" under Power Adapter should be set to Never with the "Display sleep" being set to a smaller number, like 20 or 30 minutes (many companies have security policies that govern this setting, so if you are setting Lion Server up at a company, verify that your choices meet your security requirements). Additionally, uncheck the "Put the hard disk(s) to sleep when possible" box and check the "Restart automatically if the computer freezes" box (Figure 2-4).

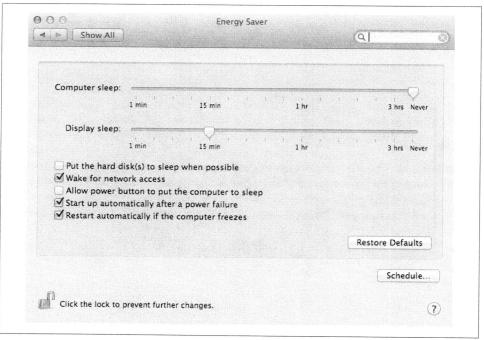

Figure 2-4. Configuring power management

If you are using an uninterruptable power supply (UPS) with your server and connect it to the server via USB, then you should also be able to use the Battery tab to configure how quickly the server shuts down when the battery goes off (check with the manual of the vendor who makes the UPS for more information on configuration).

Installing the Server Software

Once the server's name and IP address are properly configured and the server isn't going to go to sleep at just the moment when you need to transfer that one big file for the day, it's time to install the server software. To do so, open the App Store and search for Lion Server. Click on OS X Lion Server and purchase the app.

Once the Server app is installed, it will appear in the Dock. The next step is to install the components. To do so, open the Server app from the Applications folder. When opened for the first time, Server prompts you to install the components. Click on Install to complete the OS X Server installation.

Once the components are installed, install the Server Admin tools, available on the Apple website at *http://support.apple.com/kb/DL1457*. The tools will download as a standard Apple package. Run the installer, selecting the default options until the package installation is complete.

In some cases, you won't actually need the Server Admin tools, but they are great for troubleshooting and many services do require them, so they should be installed as a part of the initial Lion Server setup process.

Completing Installation Tasks

Once the Server app, its components, and the Server Admin tools are installed, you have a fully functioning server. You can then start services, configure roles that the server will fill, and use the server. But before you begin in earnest, first let's check some settings and finish some configuration options before configuring services.

Checking the Hostname (Again)

Sure, you checked the hostname. But I cannot underscore enough the importance of DNS and the name of the server. For good measure, once the server has been installed, check the hostname one more time. This doesn't have to happen at the command line, but instead we can use the newly acquired Server application.

Open the Server app from the Dock (or the */Applications* directory) and click on the Next Steps drawer toward the bottom of the screen if it is not already open. The first item in the list is Configure Network. Here, you want to see a message reading: Your network is configured properly. Or you can change network settings in the Server pane if the server's name is not properly configured (Figure 2-5).

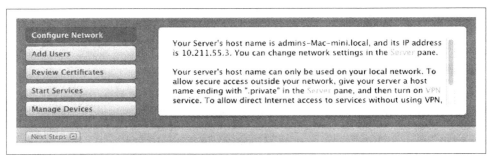

Figure 2-5. Network installation tasks

If the network is not configured properly, DNS would have been installed by default. The DNS server, configured using Server Admin rather than the Server app, is covered in Chapter 9. But if you see an entry in the DNS zones in Server Admin for the server, note that the entry is automatically generated any time that the server's forward and reverse DNS are not in alignment with the hostname. If you wish to change the hostname at this point, rather than use scutil, click on the name of the server in the Server application's sidebar and then click on the Network tab (Figure 2-6).

Here, clicking Edit invokes a wizard that can be used to change the name of an OS X Server. If you change the name, then it is worth noting that the SSL certificate will likely reference an invalid hostname.

Setting up SSL

SSL (Secure Sockets Layer) is a technology used to secure network traffic. Using SSL with services increases the security of those services drastically. Although not required for most services, the security benefits of SSL mean that you will want to use SSL with as many services as possible.

Each server has an SSL certificate installed during the installation of OS X Server. These certificates are self-signed and by default are fully functional with the services provided for the most part. However, in many cases, it is worthwhile to install your own new certificate, as the one that is present might not be correct (e.g., if the hostname for the server was different at the time the certificate was created). To do so, open the Server application and click on the name of the server in the HOSTNAME section of the Server sidebar.

Click on the Settings tab and then click on the Edit... button in the SSL Certificate field. At the drop-down menu, click on the cogwheel icon and then click on Manage Certificates..., as seen in Figure 2-7.

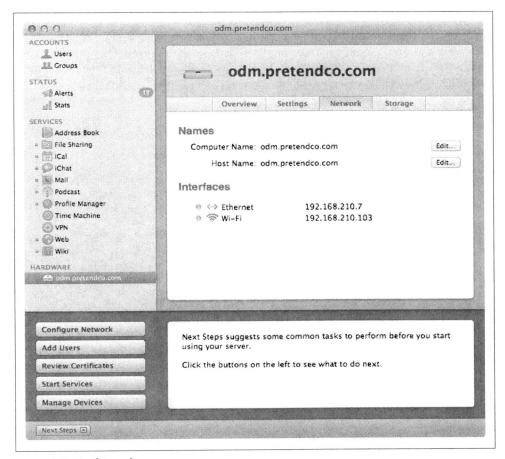

Figure 2-6. Verifying a hostname

Figure 2-7. Creating a certificate

At the Manage Certificates screen, click on the plus sign ("+") and then click on Create a Certificate Identity (unless you have purchased a certificate and you therefore have a certificate to import, then click on Import a Certificate Identity). The Certificate Assistant will then open. At the Create Your Certificate screen, provide the server's hostname in the Name field and choose "Self-Signed Root" as the "Identity Type" and "SSL Server" as the "Certificate Type." Also, leave the box for "Let me override defaults" unchecked and click on the Create button (Figure 2-8).

Figure 2-8. Configuring a new certificate

A screen will then appear asking if you want to export the certificate that was just created. Click on Always Allow here in order to allow access to the certificate.

The Server app should still be at the Settings screen for the hostname. Click on Edit beside the SSL Certificate field and at the resultant screen, click on the Certificate drop-down menu and then select the newly created certificate from the list shown. Then click on the OK button to select the certificate (Figure 2-9) and then note that the configuration settings will be written to OS X Server (indicated in the lower-right corner of the screen).

Once the certificate has been installed, clients will need to trust it. If you purchased the certificate from a certificate authority (e.g., GeoTrust or Thawte), then there will likely be nothing required to do on client systems in order for them to trust it. However, if you are using a self-signed certificate, then you will need to install it on client systems. For some services, such as Mobile Device Management (MDM is covered in Chapter 9), this is part of the setup process.

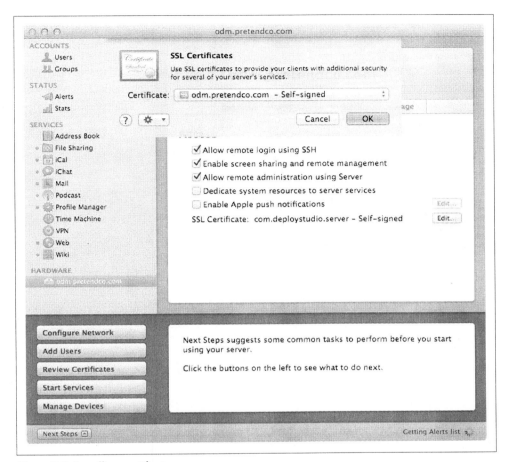

Figure 2-9. Installing certificates

Setting Date and Time

The date and time is a very important aspect of OS X Servers. Kerberos, a key element of securing authentication traffic, and other areas of the system leverage the date and timestamps to generate encryption algorithms. Client systems using time that is five or more minutes off (by default) will fail when attempting to authenticate via Kerberos, and there are other problems that can arise as well. Therefore, OS X Server acts as a network time server, using the popular open source Network Time Protocol (NTP). NTP is enabled by default, a setting that can be disabled if you'd rather use Apple's time server (set at time.apple.com from clients and servers by default) or one other than the server (e.g., if you have multiple servers).

To disable NTP serving, open Server Admin (installed previously in this chapter) and click on the name of the server in the SERVERS sidebar. Then click on Settings in the Server Admin toolbar (that runs atop the screen) and uncheck the box for Network Time Server, as in Figure 2-10. The NTP services will then stop.

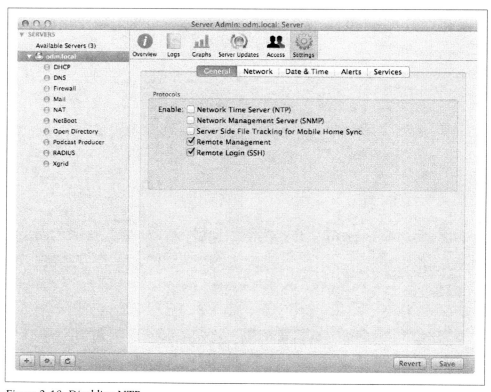

Figure 2-10. Disabling NTP

To change the NTP server that you are using on client computers or network servers, open System Preferences from the Apple menu and click on the Date & Time System Preference pane. Here, you will see that by default, clients automatically update their times. By default, time.apple.com is listed in the "Set date and time automatically" field. To change the settings to a local NTP server (or one on your network), enter the name or IP address of the NTP server you would like to use.

There is no Save button on the System Preference screens. I usually like to click on Show All to go back to the main System Preference screen and then click Date & Time again to make sure that the setting was successfully changed.

While all OS X Servers by default run NTP services, you only need one. Therefore, in most environments, you should disable NTP on all but one (or two if you would like to cluster NTP services) of the servers and then link each of the servers and clients to the newly configured NTP server.

Creating Users

Creating users can be done in the Server application or using the Workgroup Manager application. When you create a user account, it can be stored in one of two places: in the local directory service (which is comprised of flat plist files stored in */var/db/dslocal/ nodes/Default/users*) or in the Open Directory database (by default, Lion Server does not run a shared Open Directory database when installed). We'll describe using Open Directory later in this chapter, but the important thing to consider is that if you create users in the Server application before promoting a server to an Open Directory Master, the users will be created in the local database and will not be shared between servers and client computers. If you create users in Server after upgrading to an Open Directory Master, the users will automatically be placed in the Open Directory database.

To create a new user, open the Server application from */Applications*. Then, click on the Users entry under the ACCOUNTS section of the Server sidebar. Click on the plus sign ("+") and then provide the following information in the supplied fields (Figure 2-11):

Full Name
    The name of the user (e.g., Harry Seldon)
Account Name
    The short name of the user (e.g., hseldon)
Email Address
    The user's email address (e.g., *hseldon@foundationsedge.com*)
Password
    The password for the user (e.g., i<3daneel)
Verify
    Enter the password for the user again (e.g., i<3daneel)

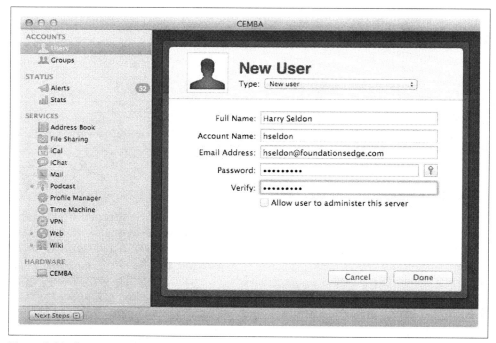

Figure 2-11. Creating user accounts

Click on the Done button when you have provided the appropriate information. Then, click on the cogwheel icon with the new account highlighted and click on Edit Access to Services. By default, all services will be enabled for the newly created user account. Here, uncheck the box for each service you do not want the user to have access to on the server (Figure 2-12).

Click the OK button once you have selected the appropriate services to complete the account setup process.

 There is no need to disable services that are not installed on the server, unless you are planning to host those services on another server within the same Open Directory domain.

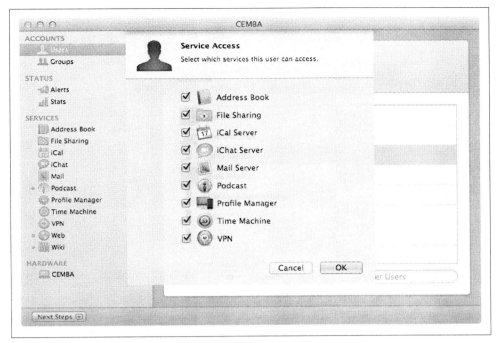

Figure 2-12. Configuring service access control lists

Creating Groups

One of the more important reasons to have users on servers is to put them in groups so that resources can be assigned to those groups. For example, when creating a file share (covered further in Chapter 3), adding multiple users to each share can be time consuming and get increasingly convoluted as time goes on and the environment becomes more complex. Instead, adding users to groups makes it easier to track access to objects, add users, and configure permissions. Whether groups exist in Open Directory or locally follows the same logic as with the user accounts. However, a local group can house Open Directory users, further complicating matters. In general, if you are going to use Open Directory accounts, it is a good idea to use Open Directory groups with them.

To create a group, open the Server application from */Applications*. Click on the plus sign to create the new group, providing a full name and group name in the respective fields (group name is the equivalent of the user account short name field). Click on Done to create the new group (Figure 2-13).

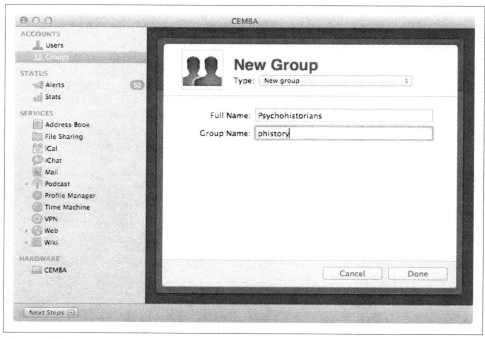

Figure 2-13. Creating a group

Adding Users to Groups

There is little reason to have a group without users in it. So let's add some. Once the group has initially been created, click on the pencil icon and then use the Members section of the screen to add and remove members. Click on the plus sign and then type the short name of a user to add to the group. While you are typing, the field will start looking to autocomplete the user's name, which can be seen in Figure 2-14. When the query finds the right account, click on the account name or just hit the Enter key.

Repeat the process by clicking on the plus sign for each user you wish to add to the group. When all of the members have been added, click on the Done button. Now that you have created your first group, it is worth mentioning that you can also manage users and groups with Workgroup manager, which we'll cover in the section "Using Workgroup Manager" on page 44 later in this chapter.

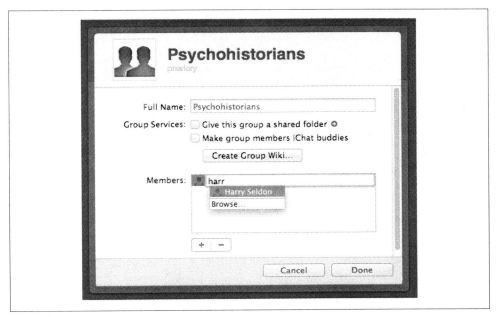

Figure 2-14. Adding users to groups

Setting Up Open Directory

Open Directory is a shared repository of users, groups, computers, and groups of computers. Open Directory has a number of options that local accounts do not have, such as a shared Kerberos repository providing single sign on (which means that when users authenticate to one service, they are authenticated to all servers and services in a given Kerberos realm). The first server in the Open Directory environment is known as the Master. Subsequent servers are then Replicas, also providing authentication and authorization services for systems that have been configured to work with Open Directory.

If you will be enabling a service that requires Open Directory, then Open Directory can be configured by that service during setup. Otherwise, if you wish to use Open Directory (e.g., you want to use mobile home folders, or user home folders that roam between machines when users log in), it can be set up manually. To do so, open Server Admin from */Applications/Server* and click on the name of the server in the SERVERS sidebar. Then, click on the Settings button in the Server Admin toolbar and the Services tab. At the list of services, check the box for Open Directory and click on Save to show it in the list of services under the server name (Figure 2-15).

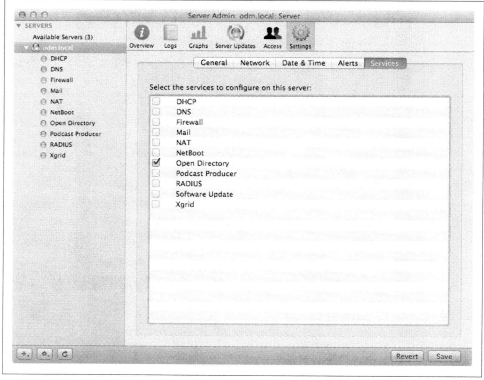

Figure 2-15. Enabling the Open Directory service

Click on Open Directory in the list of services under the server name and then click on Settings in the Server Admin toolbar and click on the General tab. The Role should initially be configured as a standalone directory, meaning that accounts are stored locally rather than shared to the domain. Then, click on the Change... button to bring up the Open Directory Assistant. At the Choose Directory Role screen, click on Set up an Open Directory master and click on the Continue button (setting up replicas will be covered later in this section).

At the Directory Administrator screen, the administrative account that has rights to manage Open Directory is configured. The Open Directory database is separate from the database of local users (in fact, those that are local have pictures from the OS X picture library and those from the directory have generic pictures with globes beside them in the Server application). Here, provide the following information:

Name

   The full name that the Open Directory administrative account will have, which by default is Directory Administrator, but could be changed to something like Edge Family Administrator

Short Name

The short name of the previously provided account (e.g., edgeadmin)

User ID

A number at or above 1,000, which should likely be left as the default value

Password

Provide the password that the Directory Administrator will use

When you are satisfied with the information for the account, click on the Continue button (Figure 2-16).

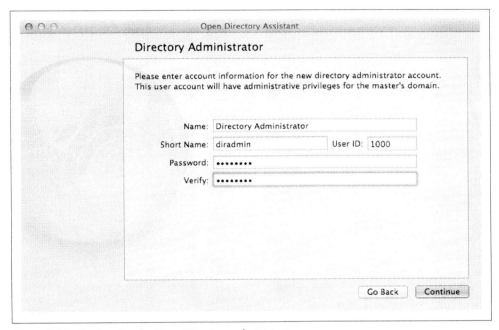

Figure 2-16. Configuring the Open Directory administrator

The Domain and Certificate Authority screen then appears. The Open Directory domain, or realm, will have an SSL certificate of its own (in addition to the certificate described earlier in this chapter) to further secure the environment. The Kerberos realm and LDAP Search Base should likely remain as they are (we will not be covering custom realm names or complicated LDAP configurations in this book). The Organization Name and CA Administrator Email fields are required and should be set to the name of your environment (e.g., The Edges) and the email for the domain (e.g., admin@krypted.com), respectively (Figure 2-17).

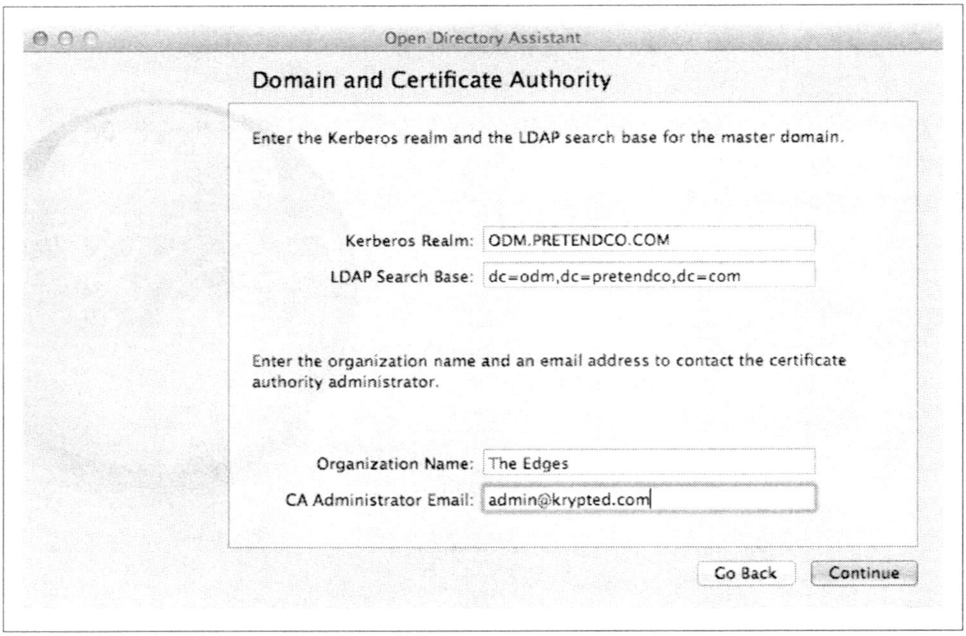

Figure 2-17. Configuring LDAP

At the Confirm Settings screen, make sure the configuration is as you wish and then click on the Continue button. Open Directory is then set up. Accounts created in the Server application will then automatically be created in the Open Directory domain. Accounts that existed prior to creating the Open Directory Master remain in the local directory service, but are still functional.

Open Directory Replicas

It is a helpful option to have a second server with the usernames and passwords available. If you have a second server, then some aspects of the Open Directory environment will still function in case the first server goes offline. Most importantly, if you are using network or mobile home directories, the clients can still authenticate to their computers.

In order to create an Open Directory Replica, the Open Directory Master must be accessible by IP or hostname and must have SSH enabled. To set up the Open Directory Replica, enable the service as you did with the Master. Once in the Server Admin sidebar, click on Open Directory under the name of the server and then click on the Change button beside the Role field, as you did with the Master.

This time, at the Choose Directory Role of the Open Directory Assistant, click on the last option in the list (Set Up an Open Directory Replica), and click Continue.

At the Replica and Certificate Authority screen, provide the following settings (Figure 2-18):

IP address or DNS name of master
Enter the IP address or the name of the Open Directory Master computer.

Domain administrator's short name
Enter the short name of the Open Directory administrative account (e.g., diradmin).

Domain administrator's password
Enter the password for the previously supplied account.

CA administrator's email
Enter the email address that was used in the CA field when configuring the Open Directory Master.

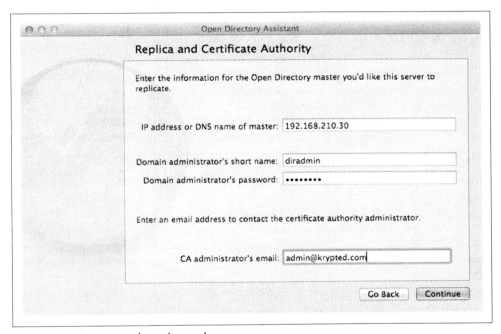

Figure 2-18. Connecting the replica to the master

Once the settings are provided, click on the Continue button and the assistant will complete. The Replica should then install, provided the prerequisites were met.

Binding to Open Directory

Once configured for Open Directory, the server announces its presence to computers on the network so they can join the domain. Users can also manually bind to the server (or be bound to the server in most cases). In order to do so, open System Preferences from under the Apple menu and then click on the Users & Groups System Preference pane. Click on the Login Options and then click on the Edit... button beside the Network Account Server field.

At the pop-up screen, click on the plus sign ("+") to be prompted for a Server. Here, provide the address (name or IP address) of the Open Directory Master (or a Replica), as in Figure 2-19.

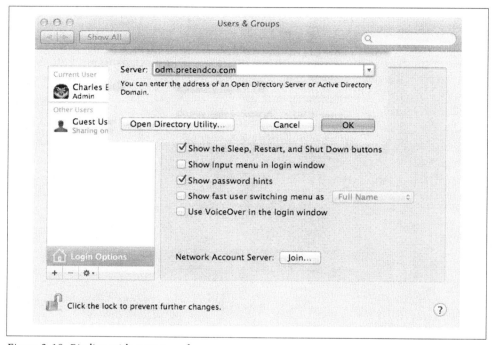

Figure 2-19. Binding with system preferences

Provided that the server has an SSL Certificate (they all should in Lion), choose "Trust the certificate" and the screen will expand to ask for a computer name, username, and password. Usually, leave the name of the computer as is and enter credentials of the directory administrator for Open Directory (Figure 2-20). Click on the OK button to complete the binding.

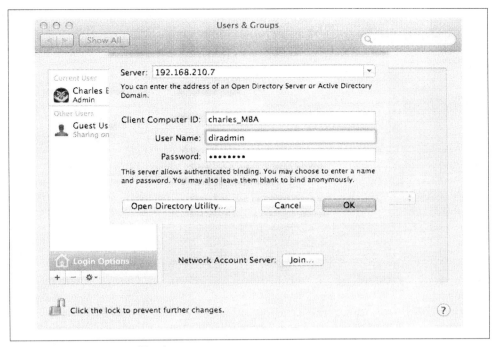

Figure 2-20. Authenticated binding

You now have the first client joined to the server domain. Next, let's look at putting some of the features of the server to use in a more managed environment.

Switching Between Directory Domains

Once a server is running as an Open Directory Master and clients can bind to it, accounts can be stored locally or in Open Directory. Both can be accessed and managed using Workgroup Manager, a tool installed with the Server Admin tools installed earlier in this chapter. Workgroup Manager is in the */Applications/Server* directory. When opened, Workgroup Manager defaults to showing the contents of the local directory service.

To switch to the Open Directory database, click on the field under the Workgroup Manager toolbar that is labeled as Viewing local directory: */Local/Default* and select the /LDAPv3/127.0.0.1 option. Doing so shows the Open Directory accounts, which by default consists only of the Directory Administrator account. This is known as switching between directory domains or domains of accounts (i.e., accounts in the local directory or Open Directory—or even Active Directory if the server is configured to work with Active Directory).

Click on the icon of the lock toward the right of the Directory Domain toolbar and then provide the username and password of the account that has administrative capabilities for that domain. You will then be able to create users, groups, and even computer accounts.

Using Workgroup Manager

Workgroup Manager also provides more granular control over accounts and lets administrators configure managed preferences, which are policies that limit what various users can do on a system. When using Workgroup manager, user creation can still be performed from within the Server app. Here, we're going to look at editing a user and simply adding a network home directory, then configuring that home directory as a portable home directory used to synchronize data in a user's home folder to the server at login and logout.

Once the Server Admin tools have been installed and users have been created, open Workgroup Manager and click on a user (this process works on groups as well). Click on the user's Home tab in the right half of the screen to see a list of home directory paths. Other than the entry for /Users, these are added by checking the "Make available for home directories" box from within each share's settings, described further in Chapter 3. Click on a network share point for a user and then click on the Save button, as can be seen in Figure 2-21. Next, click on the Create Home Now button, which populates the directory selected with the username, and within that directory, populates a standard user profile from the default user template.

Next, configure the policy for the user to make the home directory synchronize when the user authenticates. With the user highlighted, click on the Preferences button in the Workgroup Manager toolbar and then click on the Mobility icon. Each of the Managed Preferences options has options for when to manage (the field aptly called Manage). The preference itself is disabled when set to Never. Not all have the option for Once, but when they do, the setting is pushed to users, who can then alter those settings. Once settings are frequently used to push out printers, dock icons, and centralized software update services (most of the features of these having been moved into Profile Manager, which is covered further in Chapter 8).

Click on the Always radio button in the Manage field. This sets the preference to be always on. Check the box for Create mobile account when user logs in to network account (so that a cached account is created on the client computer) and then click on the Rules tab and the Home Sync subtab. Here, click on the Always radio button again and then click on the Done button, which sets the account to synchronize when the user logs in, when the user logs out, at a timed interval (defined in the Options subtab), and manually (done using a menu bar that will appear for the user's account).

The next step is to test logging in as the user who you have just enabled management for. After testing that a bound user can log in and sync their data to the server, also

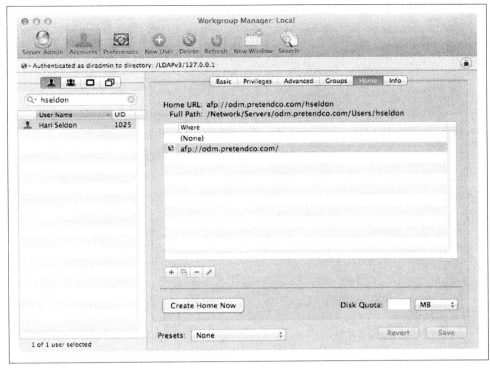

Figure 2-21. Network homes

make sure to use and test some of the other managed preferences. The purpose for each being as follows:

Applications
Allows administrators to restrict access to applications, widgets, and somewhat randomly, Front Row (OS X's built-in media browser)

Classic
Used for OS 9 compatibility; this is irrelevant in OS X Lion

Dock
Control the look, feel, and icons in the Dock

Energy Saver
Control Energy Saver settings (e.g., when the computer goes to sleep or enables a screen saver)

Finder
Force Simple Finder, remove items from the desktop, control Finder settings, and manage Finder views

Login
> Set automatic server logins, control login window settings, and limit access to computers by group

Media Access
> Restrict access to optical media (by type), internal and external drives

Mobility
> In addition to the home synchronization, as has been mentioned, also has options for enabling FileVault and expiring accounts

Network
> Define proxy server settings and centrally disable Internet Sharing AirPort (Wi-Fi) or Bluetooth

Parental Controls
> Limit access to features in OS X Server, including access to profanity in the dictionary, accessing the computer at specified times of the day, limiting who the user can communicate with through iChat, and managing the desktop experience for users

Printing
> Push and restrict access to printers

Software Update
> Sets a centralized software update server (only used in conjunction with the Software Update Server feature of OS X Server)

System Preferences
> Limits access to System Preference panes, causing them not to appear to end users

Time Machine
> Sets a centralized Time Machine Server address setting and enables Time Machine (only used in conjunction with Time Machine Server in OS X Lion Server)

Universal Access
> Automatically configures settings for disabled users (e.g., zoom, accessibility, etc.)

Finally, while we looked at controlling a user account, it is worth noting that rarely would you manage preferences on a per user basis. They can instead be managed on a group, computer, or computer group basis.

Conclusion

Installing OS X Server involves more preflight configuration than actual work. However, installing anything from the App Store depends on a zippy network connection in order to be done quickly. If you follow the steps laid out in this chapter, including the hostname and SSL preparation and postflight steps, then you should be in great shape.

Open Directory is an important aspect of OS X Server for many environments. As you now know, creating users and groups is a simple process, whether using the Server application or Workgroup Manager. The process is also basically the same whether you are using Open Directory or local accounts. The Managed Preferences offer an additional layer of features that help to automate the setup and configuration of systems as well as limit what users can do if you wish to do so.

Now that we've covered getting the server configured for the basic requirements to run services, we'll move on to configuring the #1 feature most people want in a server: the file server. And the last step in any installation should be to configure backups, which is also covered in Chapter 3 (even if you won't be using the server as a file server).

CHAPTER 3

Sharing and Backing Up Files

Once a server has been installed, it's time to start setting up the service or services that run on it. And sharing files is the most important aspect of most servers. File sharing is used to provide a centralized repository for any type of file, whether a presentation, homework, a spreadsheet used to track bills, or even a shopping list to help you remember the milk. You can then control who can open, edit, or delete files to keep each user from having inappropriate access to files and folders that are shared from the server.

There are two aspects of file sharing that are important to consider. The first is controlling access to who can do what by managing the permissions on the files. We will cover permissions first, as files do not need to be shared until the appropriate permissions have been set. The second aspect of sharing files is actually enabling the file shares and configuring settings specific to those shares.

Once we have covered setting up the server itself, we'll move on to connecting to the server from client systems. These systems include Mac OS X (Lion), iOS (iPad, iPhone, and iPod Touch), and even Windows. Each of the supported platforms uses a different protocol (by default) to connect to the server. Windows uses SMB (Samba), Mac OS X uses AFP (Apple File Protocol), and iOS uses WebDAV (Web-based Distributed Authoring and Versioning), which is based on the classic HTTP protocol so heavily used for web traffic. Finally, we'll look at Time Machine Server in this chapter. Time Machine Server is, at its core, a file share. But first, let's get the data ready to be shared to client computers by configuring the appropriate permissions.

Managing File and Folder Access with Permissions

Many environments just need to give everyone access to files and folders. This type of configuration is simplistic and typical in smaller environments. As the number of users and files grows, so too grows the complexity of the data shared by the server and the permissions for who gets access to that data. Luckily, Mac OS X comes with plenty of tools for managing who can access what, and more specifically, how that data can be accessed.

Permissions should always be configured for each user to have the least required permission to any file. This means that permissions should not be provided to any data that a user does not explicitly need access to. The easiest way to do so is to simply not include any user or group to have access to a directory that doesn't absolutely require access. Users that do not have access to the root level of a share cannot then traverse deeper into the hierarchy of files in the share. Managing access to the root of each share is done using the Server application, as discussed in "Enabling Sharing" on page 54 later in this chapter.

Once a share is created, managing permissions to files within that share is primarily done using the Finder or the Server application. Using the Command-I keystroke, or clicking on any directory or file and then choosing Get Info from the Finder's File menu brings up the Info screen. Here, permissions to files can be configured using the Sharing & Permissions section, accessible using the disclosure triangle for that section. Configuring permissions on servers and clients can be done from the Finder. But on servers, administrators can change POSIX settings more easily using the Server application.

To configure permissions using the Server application, click on the server name under the Hardware section of the sidebar. Then click on the Storage tab and click on a file or folder to change the permissions of. Then, using the cogwheel icon's contextual menu, click on Edit Permissions. As you can see in Figure 3-1, each user or group that has access to a given directory is shown, as well as what kind of privileges. The bottom three items are POSIX permissions, and all items above those are Access Control Lists, or ACLs.

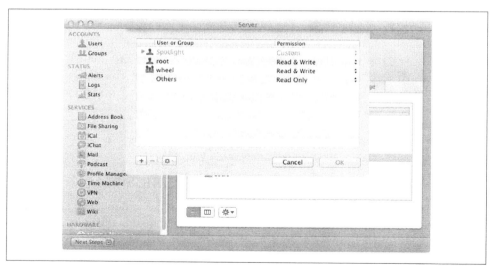

Figure 3-1. Configuring permissions using Server.app

POSIX

Portable Operating System Interface for Unix (POSIX) permissions are standards that dictate how Unix-based operating systems should function. POSIX permissions are how OS X refers to its legacy file permissions that allow OS X to be part of the Unix family of operating systems. As mentioned, the last three items listed in the Edit Permissions screen are the POSIX permissions. These include an Owner, a Group, and Everyone. The owner can be any user on the system, the group can be any group on the system, and Everyone includes all authenticated users.

The permissions for Owner, Group, and Everyone are set using the drop-down menus next to each entry in the Finder Info screen. The settings for each are:

Read & Write
> Users have full permissions to edit, read, and even delete files.

Read Only
> Allows users to read items in the directory or open a file, but not to edit the contents. A great example of this is forms and templates. In many cases, forms and templates should only be Read & Write for a select group, such as Human Resources, and should be Read Only for everyone else.

Write Only
> Allows users to write to the folder, but not to read the contents, often used for drop boxes. For example, homework submission should be configured in such a way that a teacher or parent can read and write to the folder (thus being the Owner or Group) and Everyone can Write Only, so that students cannot see each other's work.

No Access or None
> Available only for Everyone from the Finder, No Access means users not in the Owner or Group section (or an ACL, which will be covered in the next section) have no access to even see contents of directories.

Changing permissions for a file or folder is as easy as clicking on the entry for Read & Write, Read Only, or Write Only and selecting the replacement. While the POSIX permissions that can be configured from the Finder are somewhat limited, the command-line options available allow for much more granular permissions. For example, using the chmod command, execute only can be configured or No Access can be applied to groups and even owners of files and folders.

The entries for Owner and Group are typically set when a share is created. These can also be changed at any point using the Server app or the command line. To change the name in the Server app, double-click on the entry for the Owner or Group. Then type the short name of the Owner or Group you would like to use. Click out of the screen to then commit these changes and the new settings will be effective immediately. Use the cogwheel icon again to bring up the Propagate Permissions option, in order to push these changes down to subfolders and files.

The chown command is used to set either the Owner or the Group. While the command line may seem daunting at first, few commands are easier than chown. To change the owner, use chown followed by the user or group who should become the Owner or Group and then the location to change the ownership for (e.g., the file or directory). For example, to change the Group for */Shared/Assignments* to a group called Teachers (where Teachers is the short name for the group), use the following command:

```
chown Teachers /Shared/Assignments
```

Or if there are already items in the directory that also need their permissions changed, add the -R option to recursively make these changes:

```
chown -R Teachers /Shared/Assignments
```

If you get any errors indicating that the operation is not permitted, then you will need to run the command with elevated privileges, which means you'll need to preface it with the sudo command:

```
sudo chown -R Teachers /Shared/Assignments
```

Once the permissions have been set for a single folder, you could also elect to make those changes recursive using the Info screen in the Finder. To do so, browse to the directory in the Finder, use Command-I or the Get Info option under the File menu, and then (provided the permissions are set as intended), click on the icon of the cogwheel to bring up a menu. In that menu, click on "Apply to enclosed items..." and provide the administrative username and password when prompted.

In case you're not interested in using the command line to manage POSIX permissions, consider getting an application called BatChmod. BatChmod gives you the ability to manage POSIX permissions as granularly as you would like in a simple to use graphically appealing interface. BatChmod an be obtained at *http://www.lagentesoft.com/batchmod/index.html*.

ACLs

Now that we've looked at managing POSIX permissions, let's look into ACLs, which most administrators will use more, given their flexibility. ACLs are a slightly different beast. Each entry in the ACL is known as an access control entry (ACE). You can have a lot of these entries, whereas you can only have the three objects for POSIX permissions. ACLs also provide a lot more types of permissions, including each of the following for the user or group specified in the ACE for files and/or folders:

Administration
    Settings that allow users to change permissions of objects themselves

Change Permissions
    Can change permissions

Change Owner
    Can change the owner (therefore taking ownership)

Read
    Settings limiting access to read options

Read Attributes
    Can read POSIX attributes (e.g., modification date)

Read Extended Attributes
    Can read extended attributes (e.g., metadata such as quarantine status)

List Folder Contents (Read Data)
    Allow listing the contents of a directory or file

Traverse Folder (Execute File)
    Allows opening the folder in order to get to a subfolder as well as executing any
    files in the folder as a program

Read Permissions
    Allow reading permissions that are applied to the object

Write
    Settings limiting access to write options

Write Attributes
    Allows modifying the file or folder (e.g., modification date)

Write Extended Attributes
    Allows writing extended attributes (e.g., metadata such as quarantine status)

Create Files (Write Data)
    Allows creating files inside the directory

Create Folder (Append Data)
    Allows creating a new directory inside the directory

Delete
    The right to delete the object and delete subfolders

Files
    The right to delete objects within the object

Inheritance
    Settings that control how permissions are applied to new objects

Apply to this folder
    ACEs are applied to the directory

Apply to child folders
    ACEs are applied to subfolders but not to the directory

Apply to child files
    ACEs are applied to files within the directory

Apply to all descendants
    ACEs are applied to all new objects within the directory

For each entry, select the minimum permissions required for each user or group. Make
sure to use groups where possible (even, in some cases, if there is only one user in a

group). Using the Full Control option in the drop-down list will enable all of the checkboxes, allowing users who have Full Control to do anything they like with the files and folders. By using a few groups, you can then very granularly limit access to files and folders. For example, let's say you have a group called Teachers, another called Students, and yet another called Staff. Let's say you want Teachers to have Full Control over files, Students to have Read Only access, and Staff to have access to Create but not Delete. You could easily achieve that with three ACEs, checking the appropriate boxes for each group provided.

 Recursively changing permissions does not remove ACEs from items further down in the hierarchy that aren't a collision with new items being propagated. If a hierarchy becomes too complicated and you just want to remove all ACEs and start anew, use chmod with the -R and -N options followed by the directory path, and all ACEs will be removed from that directory as well as all subdirectories:

```
chmod -RN /Shared/Homework
```

Enabling Sharing

Once the permissions are appropriately set for data being shared, it's time to set up file sharing and create each share. To do so, open the Server application from */Applications* and then click on the File Sharing entry in the sidebar. Here, click on each share that you won't be using and then click on the minus sign ("-") to disable it (the data stays intact in its original location if there was any).

Once any shares that aren't needed have been removed, click on the ON and OFF switch (Figure 3-2) to enable the service. This enables both the AFP and SMB protocols to accept network connections, which are then enabled and disabled per share.

To create new shares, click on the plus sign ("+") and choose the folder to be shared, clicking on the Choose button while the folder is highlighted. The new share is then created and appears in the Share Points list. Click on the new share and then click on the pencil icon to see the settings applied to the share. The first item is the permissions to the share, configured previously in the section "Managing File and Folder Access with Permissions" on page 49. Additionally, in the Settings portion of the screen, the following options are provided (as seen in Figure 3-3):

Share with Mac clients (AFP)
   Enables AFP so clients running OS X can access the share

Share with Windows clients (SMB)
   Enables SMB so clients running Windows can access the share

Share with iOS devices (WebDAV)
   Enables WebDAV so iOS clients can access the share

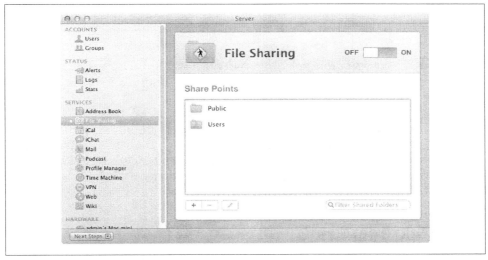

Figure 3-2. Configuring file sharing using Server.app

Allow guest users to access this share
Enables guest access for AFP, SMB, and FTP

Make available for home directories
Publishes the mount into Open Directory, which is then used as a home directory option for OS X clients (multiple shares can be used for home directories)

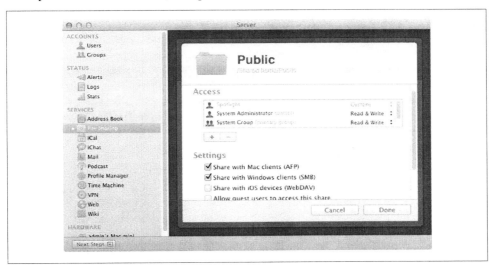

Figure 3-3. Creating file shares using Server.app

Only check the boxes required. For example, if all of your users run iOS, then there is no need to enable AFP or SMB. On the other hand, if all of the users run OS X except a few who access the server from Windows, only enable SMB on the share that the Windows users access. Also, even in home environments, it is a good idea to disable Guest access to the server.

Finally, only enable home directories for shares that will house home directories. It is a bad idea to mix home directory data with, for example, centralized shares. Therefore, make a share specifically for home directories. It is possible to have subfolders act as home directory shares; however, for ease of administration, we recommend using one share per home directory share. We also recommend grouping users into each share in a fashion where they can be managed by group. For example, in a school environment, we often recommend graduation year. This way, at the end of each year, the share can be retired (possibly after tape archival) and only the students in each graduation year will be impacted.

Connecting from Clients

By now you're probably thinking this is all pretty easy. Sure, we threw a little command line at you, but we also provided graphical means to achieve most of the same ends. Connecting client computers to shares is even easier than setting up the server portion of the shares. Each platform that connects to OS X is going to have a different way to do so. We're going to look at using AFP to connect from Mac OS X, using SMB to connect from Windows, and WebDAV to connect from iPads, iPod Touches, and iPhones.

Configuring AFP Connections from Mac OS X

A Mac can tap into an OS X Server using any of the three services: AFP, SMB, or WebDAV. However, using AFP is going to be the most native means to access file servers of any ilk, including those running on OS X Server. When accessing shares from a Mac, you can specify which protocol to use in the address that is entered. If no protocol is specified, then OS X will by default use AFP (see, it is already the most native protocol).

The simplest way to connect to an AFP share is to use the sidebar from any Finder screen. In smaller networks, servers accessible to the client will appear (a result of Bonjour). Highlight the server and any network shares that are accessible to guests will appear, as well as buttons to Connect As... and Share the screen of the server (Figure 3-4). Click on Connect As... to establish a connection to the server, and when prompted, provide a valid username and password using the Registered User field. Use the "Remember this password in my keychain" checkbox to keep the password in the keychain of the current user's profile. Then click on the Connect button and the list of shares in the Finder screen will change to include all the newly authenticated user has access to.

To connect to an AFP share manually, use the Go menu from the Finder and click on Connect to Server (or Command-K if you want to use keystrokes). At the Connect to Server screen, enter the name of the server in the Server Address field. Once entered, use the plus sign ("+") to add the server into the list of Favorite Servers (very helpful to users that access the server frequently). Remove servers from the Favorite Servers list by highlighting them and then clicking on the Remove button. Once the entry is in the Favorites, click on the Connect button to establish a connection to the server.

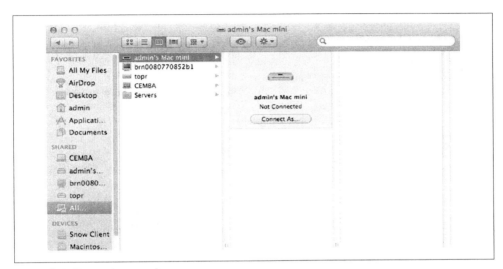

Figure 3-4. Connecting to a share

Connecting from Windows

Setting up Mac clients is about as easy as you get. But as mentioned earlier, Windows computers can connect to the Mac OS X Server as well, using SMB. To establish a connection from a Windows computer, let's begin by clicking on the Windows icon (aka the Start menu) and then typing run in the Search programs and files field. Provided the Run program is the first item to appear in the list of found applications, click on it or simply hit the Enter key.

At the run dialog, provide the computer with the IP address or name of your server (if names don't work you should always be able to just use the IP address) preceded by a \\ as can be seen in Figure 3-5.

If the computer finds the server, you will then be prompted for the username and password at the Network Password field. If you would like for the computer to remember the password, click on the Remember Password checkbox. Enter the username and password from the server that you would like to use and then click OK.

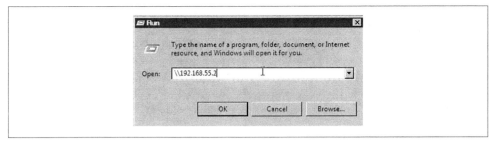

Figure 3-5. Connecting from Windows

If the password works, you should then be looking at a list of shares that the account that authenticated has access to. If you are only connecting one time, you can go ahead and double-click to open each. However, if you will be connecting frequently, then go ahead and right-click on the share and select the option "To map a network drive." At the Map Network Drive screen, choose a drive letter (usually toward the end of the alphabet is a good choice, as the letters at the beginning of the alphabet are typically used for disk drives connected directly to the computer). Once you have picked a drive letter, click on the Finish button. Then use the sidebar of any Windows Explorer screen to choose the newly mapped drive under the Computer section as seen in Figure 3-6.

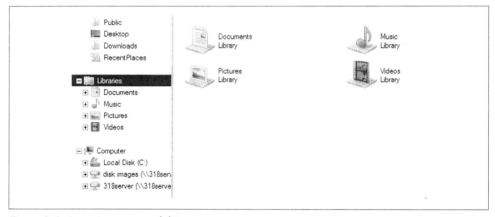

Figure 3-6. Accessing a mapped drive

 Use the `net use` command to map drives from the command line in Windows.

Configuring WebDAV Connections from iOS

There are a number of AFP and/or SMB clients for the iPad and iPhone. But the future of iOS is all about WebDAV. WebDAV is a set of file sharing methods based on the same protocol that powers the Web: HTTP. Apple loves web standards (as you'll notice when we look at iCal and Address Book servers), and seems to be dropping support for traditional file sharing protocols (e.g., FTP and NFS) in favor of newer web-based protocols, including WebDAV. Previously, we looked at setting up a share to work via WebDAV. Here, we will look at configuring an iPhone to access a WebDAV share.

While the future is bright for WebDAV, iOS doesn't currently support WebDAV natively. In other words, you need "an app for that." A quick search for WebDAV on the App Store in iOS results in a number of results. For this example, we're going to use the free app, WebDAV Nav. To use it to connect to a share, do a search on the App Store, then download, install, and open WebDAV Nav. Once open, click on the plus sign ("+") and then provide:

Name
> A simple name to remember the server by, such as Edge Home Server in Figure 3-7

Server URL
> Address (name or IP address) to access the server, in the form of *http://SERVER-NAME/webdav*, where the *SERVERNAME* is the name of the server you want to connect to

Username
> The username to access the server with

Password
> The password for the username provided in the Username field

Once ready, click Save to commit these changes. Then tap on the name of the server provided to see a list of shares and the data within the shares. You can then open files with apps and save files to the clipboard and paste them into the file server as needed.

 Pages can connect directly with WebDAV using the Same URL.

Logging in Remotely

Connecting to a file server from outside the network that server resides in can be as easy or as complicated as security policies allow. If you don't mind connections being made directly to the server from outside of the firewall, then one need only forward a port (or some ports) from the IP that comes into the environment to the server. Doing so is a feature built into every router sold and is usually as easy as editing an access

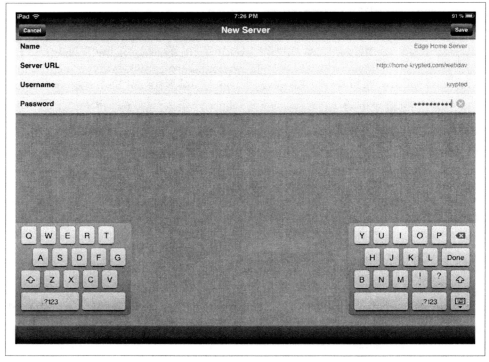

Figure 3-7. Connecting from an iPad with WebDAV NAV

control list of some sort. But before doing so, it is important to know what ports need to be forwarded.

Apple servers can use a variety of ports. AFP, SMB, and WebDAV all use different ports because they are different protocols. By default, AFP uses port 548, SMB uses port 445, and WebDAV uses port 80. These aren't constants though. For example, the AFP port can be changed to 549 using the following `serveradmin` command:

```
serveradmin settings afp:afpTCPPort = 549
```

For further information on which ports are used in various scenarios, see the Well Known TCP and UDP Ports Used By Apple Products knowledge base document TS1629 (*http://support.apple.com/kb/ts1629*).

Backing Up

One of the most important aspects of centralizing your data into a single system is to make sure that the server is protected. Time Machine is free and built into each and every OS X Lion computer, including OS X Server. In this section, we will look at using Time Machine to back up a server and the clients that use the server (e.g., to grab those iTunes and iPhoto libraries that are stored locally on each computer).

Backing Up the Server

Time Machine is not the best backup program ever conceived. But in addition to being free, Time Machine is incredibly easy to configure. In some cases, you will outgrow Time Machine. For example, you will want to have a copy of your data on tape, which Time Machine doesn't work with. Or you may look to perform cloud-based backups, which Time Machine isn't engineered for. But for most companies, Time Machine will work perfectly well to back up the operating system itself.

Configuring Time Machine to back up a server is similar to using Time Machine to back up a client computer. To begin, open System Preferences from the Apple menu and then click on the Time Machine System Preference pane. As you can see in Figure 3-8, there are only three buttons in the System Preference pane. Let's start by clicking on the Options button.

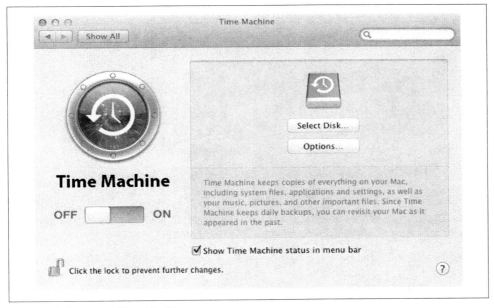

Figure 3-8. Setting up Time Machine

When clicked, the Options button shows a list of items to exclude from backups in the "Exclude these items from backups" section, which can be seen in Figure 3-9. Here, click on the plus sign ("+") to add directories to those that you do not want to back up. This brings up a standard browse dialog; select any directories that you specifically do not need to back up and then click on Exclude to add directories to the list (for the purposes of this example, we're not going to exclude any items). There are also three checkboxes on the screen. These include:

Back up while on battery power

Continues to back up, even when the system is not connected to a power source and is running on battery power (primarily for laptops, but also useful in environments with surge protectors). This option is almost universally a good idea to enable.

Notify after old backups are deleted

Informs users when old files are removed from the backups. This option is almost always a good idea as well.

Lock documents after last edit

Sets the Versions setting for documents to locked after the time indicated in the field. This option is not pertinent to servers, as Versions data is saved to local computers rather than on servers.

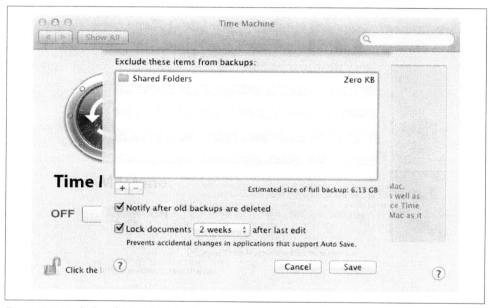

Figure 3-9. Excluding folders from backups

In our example, we have configured no exclusions from our backups and left all three of the checkboxes checked (Figure 3-10). Click on the Save button to configure Time Machine with the changes that best work for you. Next, click the ON button and the Select Disk option will appear. Here, simply choose the volume that you will back up to. In this example, our volume is a USB disk formatted in one partition called TMServer. Once selected, click on Use Backup Disk.

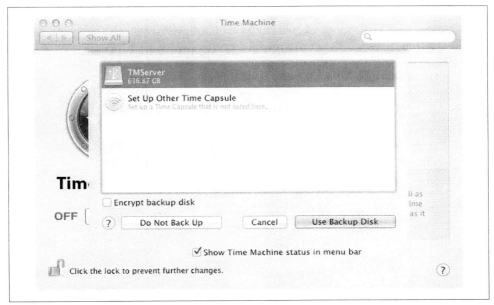

Figure 3-10. Selecting a volume to use with Time Machine

Backups will wait 120 seconds from when the Use Backup Disk button is clicked before they will start. Once started, the Apple menu for Time Machine will then show that backups are in progress and when clicked, the Time Machine System preference pane will show the oldest, the most recent, and the time the next backup is scheduled.

Once backed up, data is restored using the Time Machine application, or booting to a Recovery partition and choosing to perform a Time Machine restore (e.g., bare metal restores).

Backing Up Open Directory

Now that there's a solid backup of the data that is unreproducible in the event of a failure, let's turn our attention to getting to a point where we can restore any items that are often not restorable from within Time Machine, starting with all of the usernames and passwords created on the server in Open Directory.

One way to keep a good backup of Open Directory is to export settings after setting up new accounts. Backing up Open Directory is done manually using Server Admin. Once new accounts are created in Workgroup Manager or Server, open Server Admin from */Applications/Server*. Then click on the Open Directory service in the Server Admin SERVERS sidebar. Clicking Archive in the Server Admin toolbar then brings up the screen used to export the contents of Open Directory.

Click on the Choose button to bring up a standard OS X browse dialog. Here, browse to the folder that you would like to back Open Directory up to. Then click on the Archive button (Figure 3-11) to run the backup.

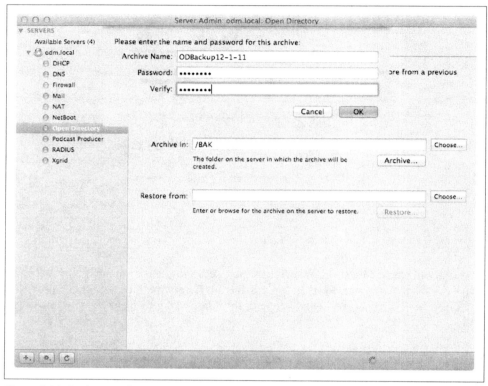

Figure 3-11. Backing up Open Directory

When prompted, provide a password that will be used to restore the backup when needed. Restoring backups is then performed by using the Choose button in the "Restore from" section of the Open Directory Restore screen and choosing the file, providing the same password when prompted.

Backups should always be automated. Especially if a lot of accounts are being added and removed from Open Directory, causing daily change in the Open Directory database. In order to facilitate automating the backup of Open Directory, consider using 318's Open Directory Auto Archiver, available at *http://techjournal.318.com/scripts/open-directory-auto-archiver*. This package will automatically configure the server to back up Open Directory databases on a nightly basis, likely saving you considerable time scripting your own backups.

Provided that Open Directory backups are in flat files and their directory is not excluded from backups, they will then be backed up in the standard Time Machine backups for the rest of the computer.

Backing Up Server Configurations

A server can take a long time to set up. And once set up, it can take even longer to get the settings exactly as they were in the event of a crash. Time Machine is great for many things, but restoring settings for a server is not one of them, unless doing a full system restore. Therefore, it's always a good idea to have a layered approach to backups, one layer being to restore the server to working order in the event of corruption to a service configuration. In order to do so, one must first have a backup of service settings that can be restored on a service-by-service basis.

Each service has a built-in set of command-line options used to list, back up, and even restore the service's settings. Service settings can be backed up from Server Admin, using the Export -> Service Settings item in the Server menu; however, only service settings for services shown in Server Admin are backed up here. Services that are configured in the Server app do not get backed up by exporting service settings. Therefore, to back up a service's settings, the serveradmin command can be used. Simply run serveradmin followed by the settings verb and then the name of the service whose settings should get backed up. The output of this command is then passed into a text file used to back up the service settings using the > followed by the name of the file to pass the settings into. For example, to back Address Book Server settings up into a file called *addressbook.settings*, use the following command:

```
sudo serveradmin settings addressbook > addressbook.settings
```

By running this command nightly, per service, one could automate the backup of each service's settings. But because we're strong proponents of backing up settings and data as often as possible, and because we're not fans of telling people they need to write scripts, we recommend using a program called SABackup (*http://sabackup.sourceforge .net/*) to automate backing up service settings on a nightly basis.

Backing Up Client Workstations

Apple has a couple of great devices in the AirPort and Time Capsule. Both can be used for shared storage, providing a centralized repository for files and backups through Time Machine. The two are very similar, with the main exception being that the Time Capsule has a built-in drive, whereas AirPorts require a USB drive to provide shared storage (a USB drive can also be used with Time Capsule either to back it up or to extend the amount of storage provided).

Both are much more limited compared to an OS X Server; however, there is one feature that, until Lion, they could do that OS X Server could not: Time Machine Server. In OS X Lion, the same functionality was brought into OS X Server in the form of Time

Machine Server. You can back up to OS X Server without Time Machine Server, but provided you are on the same subnet, Time Machine Server actually shows the server in the list of available Time Machine targets without any additional work on the clients. Additionally, clients do not need to run a command-line hack each in order to back up to the Time Machine Server as they would if you were just backing up to a traditional AFP or SMB share.

Setting Up Time Machine Server

Setting up Time Machine Server has become one of the easiest things to do in Mac OS X Server. To do so, open the Server app and click on the Time Machine service. As with Time Machine itself, there aren't a lot of options here, as can be seen in Figure 3-12.

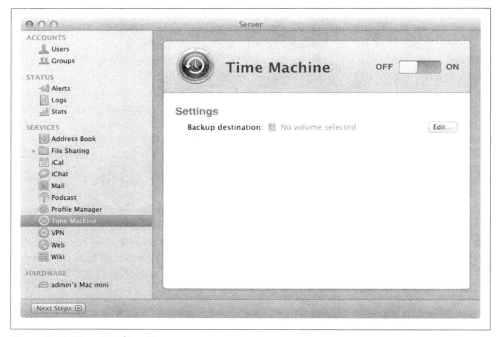

Figure 3-12. Time Machine Server

Click on the ON and OFF switch to enable Time Machine Server. The "Choose destination volume for client Time Machine backups" will then appear (Figure 3-13).

Click on the drive you want client computers to use for backup, and then click on the Use for Backup button. A share called Backups will then appear in File Sharing and be registered in Bonjour in such a way that the share will appear automatically for clients when they are configuring Time Machine.

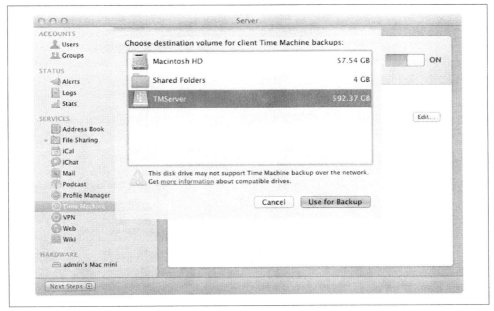

Figure 3-13. Choosing a target for Time Machine server backups

Setting Up Time Machine Server Clients

Once the server is configured, Time Machine Server clients are configured using the Time Machine System Preference pane. To set up a client, first open System Preferences from the Apple menu in OS X. Then click on the Time Machine System Preference pane. Once open, click the ON switch, and at the Select Disk screen, choose the entry for the newly created Time Machine Server, as seen in Figure 3-14.

Once selected, click on Use Backup Disk. You will then be prompted for the username and password used to authenticate to the server. Provide those credentials and click on OK. Then click on Options and define any exclusions you may have.

If the Time Machine Server does not show up, make sure you are on the same network as the server. As Time Machine Server relies heavily on the use of Bonjour, it is critical to make sure that Bonjour services work properly. An easy way to do so is checking to see if the server appears in the sidebar of an OS X client. If you are on the same network, then Time Machine Server should work great.

You can also back up using a mounted AFP or SMB share. This is often preferable when using Network Attached Storage not made by Apple or when Bonjour does not show the Time Machine Server in the list of available backup targets. When backing up to an AFP or SMB share, the shares will not appear as an available backup target automatically, even while mounted. In order to correct this, use the following command,

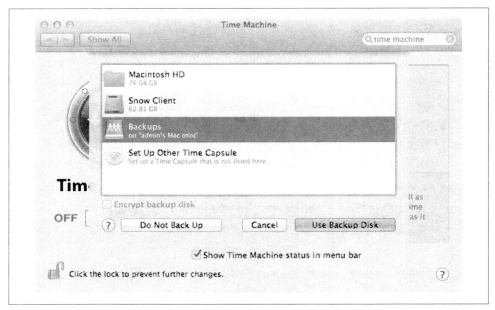

Figure 3-14. Configuring Time Machine Server clients

which uses defaults to write a boolean TMShowUnsupportedNetworkVolumes key set to True into com.apple.systempreferences.plist:

```
defaults write com.apple.systempreferences
    TMShowUnsupportedNetworkVolumes 1
```

You can also push Time Machine Server settings to clients en masse. The easiest way to do so is using Profiles, which are described further in Chapter 8.

Backing Up with Other Solutions

While Time Machine Server is a great addition to the family of products, it has its limitations. It backs up everything that changed hourly, lacks true deduplication, doesn't have granular policy-drive management, and of course, Time Machine cannot back up to tape. While Time Machine will be a great tool for many a home and small office, it just doesn't cut the mustard for larger environments.

One option that many environments are starting to rely on is cloud-based backups. Time Machine doesn't back up to the cloud. There are a few ways to shoehorn Time Machine into a cloud backup tool, but the logic built into Time Machine is very different than the logic in a cloud-based backup tool. One such tool is Carbonite, which can back up client computers and restore data to Carbonite. Other tools (e.g., Backblaze, SugarSync, and CrashPlan) also backup to cloud-based storage. Each of the tools referenced has similar features and pricing, with a little more money going toward more features and a little less toward fewer.

There are also a number of other more traditional backup tools that have clients for Mac OS X. Some tools only have backup clients for Mac OS X, such as the large enterprise management tools that include Symantec's Backup Exec and EMC's Networker. Other tools have full-fledged servers for Mac OS X, products that include Bakbone, Tolis's BRU, Archiware's PresSTORE, and Atempto's Time Navigator. These are capable of managing large tape arrays for enterprise-level (i.e., complicated) backup servers running in Mac OS X.

While these products are all very much outside the scope of file server options in OS X, it is worth mentioning them, as they provide the upgrade path once you outgrow the likes of Time Machine. In the event you find yourself needing to upgrade, review all your options and then make an informed decision based on cost, features, and of course which one you feel the most comfortable managing long term.

Conclusion

A single Mac OS X Server configured with good hardware can handle around 300 connections from users. That's on the high end. On the low end, a mini server should be able to handle between 15 and 25 concurrent users, depending on which type of files are being accessed and the protocols used to access those files. As we've shown in this chapter, OS X Server comes with a number of features—from managing permissions to controlling shares and backing up data—that make OS X Server a great file server for practically any platform.

As you can tell from how much time we spent looking at it, one of the most critical aspects of centralizing data is backing up that data. Time Machine makes for a great tool to get your data backed up regularly to disks. Time Machine also leverages the file services in OS X Server to take that backup and extend it to users on the network in the form of Time Machine Server. This new feature marks a great new feature in OS X Server, and best of all, can be pushed to users using Profiles, as we'll show in Chapter 8.

File services are one of the most common requirements for any server, and a critical aspect to many a workflow. Now that we've looked at enabling our first services in OS X Server (AFP, SMB, WebDAV, and Time Machine Server), let's turn our attention to sharing a different type of data. In Chapter 4, we will move on to shared contacts, calendars and instant messaging, often referred to as "groupware."

Sharing Address Books, Calendars, and iChat

You're heading out to the airport but remember that you need the name or address of the hotel you're staying in. Luckily, you remember that you put the address in your address book. You look at your phone to check your calendar to get the name of the hotel and grab the address from your address book. Then you map the route to the hotel from the airport. Crisis averted. Luckily, your partner was kind enough to enter all this information into your schedule, so you fire up iChat to say thanks. All of this is made possible by groupware.

Groupware has gone from a weakness to a strength in the Apple server platform in the past few releases. Most consider groupware to include shared contacts, calendars, instant messaging, and mail. The first three are covered in this chapter, whereas mail servers are covered in Chapter 5. Setting up these services is just the first part. Setting up the clients is the second. In this chapter, we'll also look at using Address Book as the Apple client for contacts, iCal for calendaring, and iChat for instant messaging.

Sharing Address Books

Address Book is the default application used for storing contacts in OS X. The Address Book application stores, manages, and shares your contacts between multiple computers and devices. Each contact is stored in a separate file. That file is synchronized to a server and then synchronized down to other client computers. Synchronization is managed using CardDAV, based on WebDAV. CardDAV stores contacts in vCards.

Before you start using any of the services in OS X Server, first complete the Next Steps items in the Server application. To start the Address Book server, open the Server application and then click on the Address Book entry in the SERVICES list. Click the ON button to start the Address Book service. The server will load for a time and a green light will then appear beside the Address Book service indicating the service is fully started.

The Directory

The Address Book server service is used to share contacts between multiple devices. But these contacts are used with a single account. Some choose to use a second account to share contacts between a few users, just using the same username and password to install the secondary account. However, this is error-prone, lacks accountability, and while it might work for a while, just isn't how the server is intended to be used. Sharing contacts between accounts is meant to be done using LDAP rather than CardDAV.

Global address lists, referenced as The Directory, are contacts available to all users in an OS X environment. These lists are then accessible to everyone in a server environment. The "Include directory contacts in search" checkbox (Figure 4-1) enables shared contacts. Said checkbox is greyed out and not an option until the server has been made into an Open Directory server, the configuration of which is covered in Chapter 2.

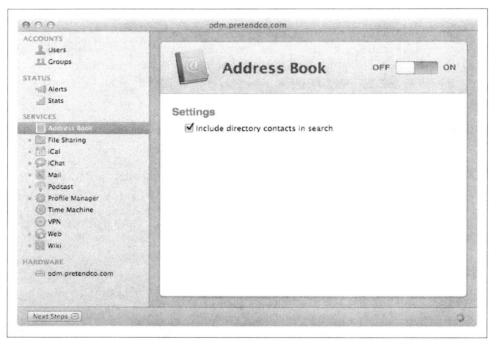

Figure 4-1. Enable the directory

Personal Address Books

Address Books aren't always shared. When you configure the Address Book client in OS X, all local contacts are by default stored in the *~/Library/Application Support/ AddressBook* directory in the sqlite databases. At first glance, Address Book shows all contacts accessible on a server. There are multiple address books in many cases though.

Each address book can be seen by clicking on the red Groups icon in Address Book. These address books are then listed under the On My Mac section in the side bar (which is meant to look like the lefthand side of a book). All items listed under the On My Mac section of the Address Book are stored locally on client computers and do not get synchronized to servers.

Configuring Address Book to Connect

Items from local address books can still be shared between systems manually by dragging Address Book entries into emails or exporting items into Address Book archives. These contacts can then be imported easily on additional client systems. But OS X Server synchronizes contacts automatically, a much better solution. To configure Address Book to connect to Address Book server in OS X Server (or another CardDAV server for that matter), first open System Preferences from the Apple menu and click on the Mail, Contacts & Calendars.

From the Mail, Contacts & Calendars System Preference pane, click on the plus sign ("+") and click on Other to bring up the Choose an account type overlay (Figure 4-2). Click Add a CardDAV account and then click on the Create... button.

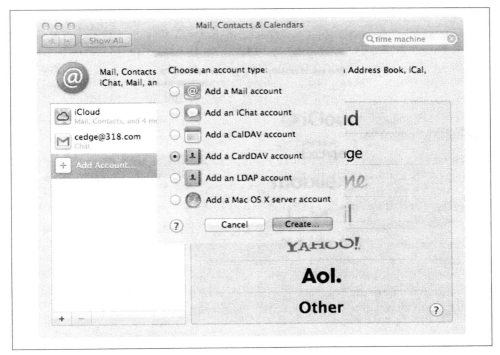

Figure 4-2. Add an account

At the Add a CardDAV Account screen, provide the username and password for a valid account of the server in their respective fields, as well as the address used to connect to the server. The server will then be shown in the sidebar discussed previously. Contacts can be dragged and dropped between local address books and shared address books and those from the server repository can be synchronized between devices.

Additionally, the LDAP store can be synchronized as well. To do so, follow the same process as with the Address Books, but instead of selecting Add a CardDAV account, choose Add an LDAP account. Directories are then shown in the sidebar under the Directories entry.

Sharing Calendars

The process for sharing calendars and connecting to the calendars is similar to that of sharing and connecting to Address Books. However, given that the iCal server has been around longer than the Address Book server, there are a few additional options. One such option is the ability to see calendars in Lion Server's web portal. Another is the ability to delegate calendars to other users, a must for collaborative calendaring. Calendaring is also more complicated because it involves locations, resources, and much more rapidly changing sets of data than contact data, which is fairly static and simple for most.

The iCal Service leverages CalDAV as a backend protocol, the big sister of the CardDAV protocol used for Address Book server. CalDAV is similar to CardDAV in that it uses files stored on a web server to manage contact events and each user has their own calendar. But given that resources can have calendars that are managed, CalDAV has a bit more logic bolted onto it and is a much more mature product offering.

Publishing Calendars

Published calendars are really helpful for very specific environments (e.g., ones in which one person disseminates calendar information to others). As with Address Book, iCal also stores local calendars in flat files. You don't have to have an iCal server to share calendars. This isn't to say that you don't need a server. Instead of iCal server, a single user can publish a calendar that others are then able to subscribe to.

To publish a calendar, from within iCal, first create a calendar to publish. Once created, click on the Calendar menu and then click on Publish... The Publish Calendar screen will provide a number of options, initially defaulting to publishing calendars to a MobileMe account in the Publish On field. If publishing to an OS X Server (we assume you are if you are reading this book), then change that field to "A private server."

When publishing to a private server, a share will need to be created. The share should be WebDAV and is indicated in the Base URL line as a standard path (for more information on WebDAV, see the section "Configuring WebDAV Connections from iOS" on page 59 in Chapter 3). Other than login information, the other options at the "Publish calendar" screen control the manner in which data is published to the calendar. These options, as seen in Figure 4-3, include the following:

Publish calendar as
> The name that will show on client computers that access the calendar

Publish on
> Whether the calendar is published to MobileMe or a private (WebDAV) server

Base URL
> The full path to access the calendar file

Login
> A username with read and write privileges to the directory that the calendar is published to

Password
> The password for the account provided in the Login field

Publish changes automatically
> When enabled, changes are automatically pushed to the published calendar; when disabled, changes are pushed manually

Publish titles and notes
> When enabled, event notes are pushed to the calendar

Publish to do items
> Pushes to-do items (e.g., from Mail's To-Do items)

Publish alerts
> When enabled, the alert items for each event are pushed to the calendar

Publish attachments
> When enabled, pushes attachments in each event to the published calendar; once configured, the calendar will be published

Once published, a URL can be distributed to users that automatically configures iCal to published calendars. Published calendars can also be subscribed to by using the Subscribe menu item in the Calendar menu and manually providing the path to the calendar. Once subscribed, the calendars can be read from by anyone with permission to access the path. In general, the WebDAV directory should be accessible as read-only by everyone except the user publishing the calendar.

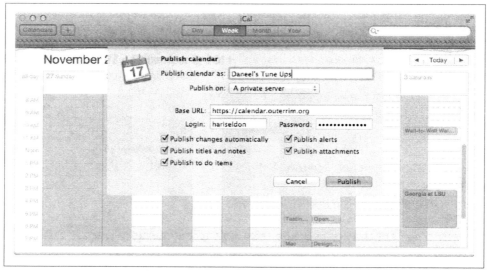

Figure 4-3. Publish calendars

Configuring iCal Server

Published calendars are really helpful for very specific environments (i.e., ones in which one person is disseminating calendar information to others). Although you don't need to have a server to share calendars, it sure gives you a lot more options, including granular control over who can access which calendars, how they can be accessed, and what can be done once accessible. But, to fully understand how much iCal server changes the game from just publishing calendars, let's turn it on and take a look.

To enable iCal Server, a server must first be running a directory service. Configure iCal Server in the Server application. But first, complete the Next Steps (see Chapter 2 for more information on doing so) section in Server. Once completed and running as a directory server, click on the entry in the Server sidebar under SERVICES for iCal.

iCal Server can send email invitations on behalf of the server. If you want the server to be able to send invitations, check the box for "Allow invitations using email addresses" and then click on the Edit button (Figure 4-4), which launches the Email address wizard. At the Configure Email Address screen, provide the email address that notifications will come from and click Next. At the Configure Server Email Address screen, configure the type of mail that the address uses. This involves filling in the incoming mail server type (IMAP versus POP), the server address, the port number, the username and the password for that address. These are typically provided by your Internet service provider or mail host. Click on the Next button once configured and then provide the address for the outgoing mail server (or SMTP server), the port number (the default setting will work unless your email host requires a separate address), the authentication type (if any), and if authentication on the SMTP server is required, then include the username and password for the email account as well. Then click on the Next button, review the Mail Account Summary screen, and click on the Finish button to complete the invitation configuration.

Then click the ON button. The service will then be configured and start. Once complete, all users in the directory service will have a calendar. If no resources are required, then the iCal client can be configured. But first, we'll look at configuring resources.

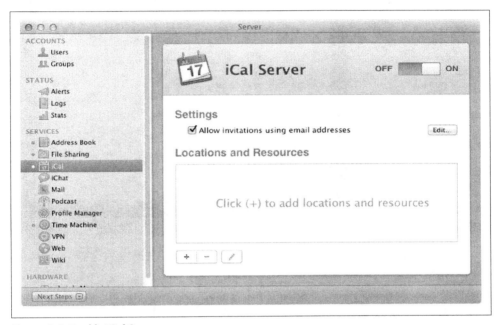

Figure 4-4. Enable iCal Server

Locations and Resources

Locations and resources are shared calendars that are accessible to multiple users. Administration of these calendars can be delegated to a user who controls that object's schedule. For example, let's say a film company rents cameras. A resource might be the camera. Or, in a school environment, an auditorium might be a location. Locations and resources are the same thing, making it a cohesive way to manage the schedules for both.

Setting up a location or resource is fairly straightforward. Once the iCal server is running, click on the service in the Server application. From the iCal Server screen, click on the icon for the plus sign ("+"). At the New Locations screen, choose a type in the Type field (the only difference is that each comes with a different icon), and then provide a name. Then choose how new invitations are treated (whether they are automatically accepted or whether the account who gets delegated administrative access over the calendar needs to approve the invitation) and then type the short name of a Delegate. Once the fields are all appropriately configured, click on the Done button (Figure 4-5).

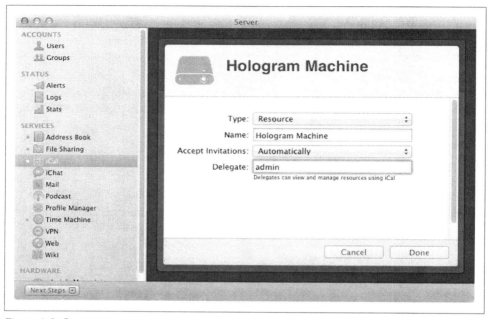

Figure 4-5. Creating resources

Once the calendars are created, they can be added to the views in iCal, which is covered in the next section.

Configuring iCal Clients

Once the server has been enabled, use the iCal application on client computers to connect to the server. Sharing calendars between users, or delegating calendars, is also done using the iCal client. By default, iCal has a number of built-in calendars (e.g., home, work, etc.). To create new local calendars, use the On My Mac menu item in the Calendar section under the File menu from within iCal. Once server client configurations have been entered, new calendars on servers can also be created using the Calendar section under the File menu and then selecting the account with which to create a new calendar for.

To set up the server client, click on the iCal menu and then click on Preferences... Then, click on Accounts under preferences. At the Accounts screen, click on the plus sign ("+") to add a new server account.

At the Add an Account screen, click on CalDAV in the Account Type menu. Then provide a username and password from the server and an IP address or server name in the Server Address field. When you are satisfied with your entry, click on Create.

The account will then be added (provided it can be accessed by the client). To test that the account has been configured properly, click on plus sign ("+") icon at the main iCal screen and add an event for the server category. You can then see in the web portal that the event is synchronizing properly between the server and the client (the web portal is explained further in the section "In the Web Portal" on page 80).

Delegated Calendars

One of the most valuable features of iCal Server is the ability for one user to allow other users access to a private calendar. The ability to have someone else schedule your appointments, to check someone else's schedule before booking a conference call, or to set up recurring events for the schedules of your colleagues is one of the main reasons to use iCal Server. As mentioned earlier, configuring clients for delegating access is done within iCal.

Once iCal has been configured to connect to a server, it is possible to delegate other users to connect to one another's calendars. To do so, open iCal from each client system. From iCal, click on the iCal menu and select Preferences... Choose the account in question and then click on the Delegation tab. Here, click on the Edit... button to give access to your calendar to others. At the Manage Account Access screen (seen in Figure 4-6), click on the plus sign ("+") icon and provide the name of the user (or email address) to give read access to the calendar(s). Use the Allow Write checkbox to allow others to edit the calendar and click on the Done button to make the changes.

Once a calendar has been shared, it needs to be added to the view in the delegated client's iCal. To do so, open iCal and click on Accounts from underneath the Preferences... menu. Then click on the account that access was delegated to and the Delegation tab. The accounts that are accessible will be shown automatically. Click on the Show checkbox for each that should be accessible and then close the Accounts screen to see the calendars listed in iCal.

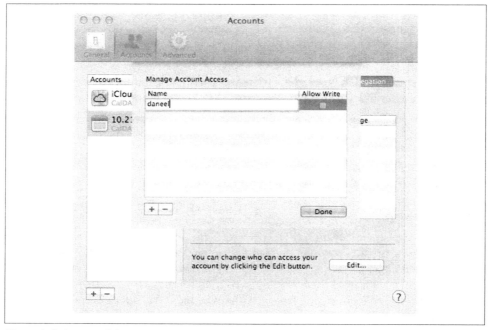

Figure 4-6. Account delegation

In the Web Portal

As mentioned, calendar synchronization is easily tested using a client and the web portal. The web portal is also helpful because you can't always be sitting at your computer; when you are in that Internet café in Paris, the web portal makes a great companion to verify you aren't missing any meetings.

The iCal web portal is automatically enabled on each website hosted on a server. We look at managing the web service further in Chapter 5. Once enabled, visit the web portal using Safari and click on Calendar (or use http://127.0.0.1/webcal from the server). From the Calendar, click on any empty time block to create a new event. The event will be created and then, provided that the iCal client has been configured on an iOS or Mac OS X device, the event will synchronize to those devices.

Configuring the Client in iOS

One of the great things about Lion Server is how well it supports iOS-based devices. And iCal Server support is among the best of the supported tools. To configure the iCal Server client in iOS, use the Settings app. From Settings, tap on the entry for Mail, Contacts, Calendars and then tap on Add Account.

At the Add Account... screen, tap on Other and then at the Calendars entry, tap on Add CalDAV Account. At the CalDAV screen, you will see a list of options, as can be seen in Figure 4-7. Here, provide the address for the server in the Server field, the short name or username of the user in the User Name field, the password of the user in the Password field, and a short indication of what the account is used for in the Description field (e.g., Home Calendar). Then tap on Next.

Figure 4-7. Setting up calendars on an iPad

The iOS device will then attempt to verify the connection to the server and if there is no SSL certificate in use, will prompt with a warning as to such. Once complete, a few advanced settings will be available using the Advanced Settings button for the account. These include whether to use SSL (an ON/OFF slider button), the port to use (which by default changes when SSL is added), and an Account URL, which allows administrators who have customized the /principals name with something different or changed the URL scheme in */etc/apache2/servermgr_web_apache2_config.plist* to still use the iOS client.

Once fully configured, open the default Calendar app included with every iPad, iPod Touch, and iPhone. Then tap on Calendars to verify that the new calendar is listed (will appear toward the bottom of the screen). Once verified, simply use the Calendar field of any new event to have the event stored on the server. The event can then be seen from any device. Hiding all other calendars will then make the default calendar set to the one on the server. In the Mail, Contacts, Calendars screen of the Settings app, there is also a Default Calendar setting (at the very bottom) that also allows you to configure which calendar to use as the default calendar.

Setting Up a Private iChat Server

Whether a small business, a school, or a household where you don't want to walk up to your kid's room to help him with algebra homework, a private iChat Server can be beneficial. iChat is the default instant messaging client for the Mac. Instant messaging allows these individuals to communicate by text, audio, and even video without leaving their chairs. This opens up the ability for receptionists to let you know that someone is waiting for you on a call or in the lobby, for teachers to send homework assignments to students, and for having a video chat with your family when you're out of town.

But most people use iChat by connecting to the AOL Instant Messenger or MobileMe networks. When publicly accessible, anyone can chat with users, whether you know them or not. Controlling who can communicate with your users can keep children safe and employees productive. This is where iChat Server is most helpful. Using iChat Server, which is based on the popular jabber open source project, you can have a private messaging solution, controlling who communicates with your users and even keeping copies of written communications.

Configuring iChat Server

The iChat Server is one of the easiest to configure. To do so, first open the Server app and click on iChat in the SERVICES section of the Server sidebar. From the iChat Server screen in Server, click the ON button. The configuration files will then be written and after a time, a green light will appear beside the iChat entry in Server.

Once the service is started, more finely grained configuration options can be set, such as linking two servers using federation, or saving copies of each chat message that is sent to and from the server.

Federation

In some cases, organizations will need to connect two servers to allow for instant messaging across, for example, two sites. Linking two iChat Servers is known as federation. Federation can also be used to link iChat Server to a number of other services, such as Google Chat. The server will need firewall ports open to do this.

To set up federation, open Server and click on iChat in the SERVERS list in the Server application's sidebar. From the iChat Server screen, click on the checkbox for Enable server-to-server federation. Then, to add the servers to federate with, click on the Edit button.

At the Server-To-Server Federation dialog box, "Allow federation with all domains" will be selected by default. Use the radio button to change this setting to "Restrict federation to the following domains." Then, use the plus sign ("+") to add each server (preferably, using the hostname if those are able to resolve), as seen in Figure 4-8.

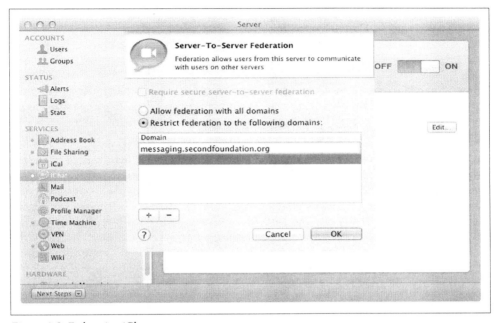

Figure 4-8. Federating iChat servers

Each server in federation will need to be added to each other server, so repeat the process on each. The "Require secure server-to-server federation" checkbox is only available as an option if you have installed an SSL certificate on the server (the certificate can be self-signed). Use this option if each server in the federated set has a certificate and if the certificate for each server is in the system keychain of each other server. SSL encryption helps to keep data secure as it is transmitted from server to server.

Saving a Copy of Each Chat

A hot topic these days is cyber-bullying in schools. One weapon used to combat cyber-bullying is to keep a transcript of conversations between students. Each iChat client can be configured to keep transcripts of conversations; however, this is not very centrally managed and in the event that users might sit at multiple computers, it can be cumbersome to track down transcripts of specific sessions. Additionally, transcripts can be deleted.

iChat Server keeps chat transcripts between users centrally. This allows you to keep a log of all instant messages. These are then indexed by spotlight and can easily be searched for offensive terms or for specific chat transcripts, and then copied or printed.

To enable centralized archival of instant messaging transcripts in iChat Server, open the Server application. Then, click on the iChat entry in Server's SERVICES section of the sidebar. Check the "Archive all chat messages" box. Messages are then stored in /Library/Server/iChat/Data/message_archives.

Setting Up the Clients

Jabber is the backend service that Lion Server uses for iChat Server. The iChat client works with AOL Instant Messenger, MSN, and Jabber. When configured, the service connects users to one another, allowing for instant messaging, video conferencing, and audio chats.

To set up a client in OS X to connect to a Jabber service, use iChat, located in /Applications. Once open, click on the iChat menu and then click on Preferences.... Click on Accounts at the Preferences screen and then click on the plus sign ("+") to create a new account. At the Account Setup wizard, select Jabber in the Account Type drop-down menu. Then provide the username and password entered in the Users section of the Server application. Click on the disclosure triangle for Server Options to bring up the fields to provide a server address and port. The address should be the name or IP address of the server and the port should, by default, be 5222 unless you check the Use SSL checkbox, in which case it is 5223 (and the server's certificate may need to be accepted).

Figure 4-9 shows the settings for a user called hariseldon on a server called messaging.outerrim.com on port 5223. You can change the ports that iChat Server uses using the serveradmin command. For example, use the following command to change iChat to use port 5000:

```
serveradmin settings jabber:jabberdClientTLS = 5000
```

Once iChat has been configured, each user will need to be added. There are ways to automatically populate the list of users that are available to iChat Server using the jabber_autobuddy command in the Terminal. For more information on doing so, see http://developer.apple.com/documentation/Darwin/Reference/ManPages/man8/jabber_autobuddy.8.html.

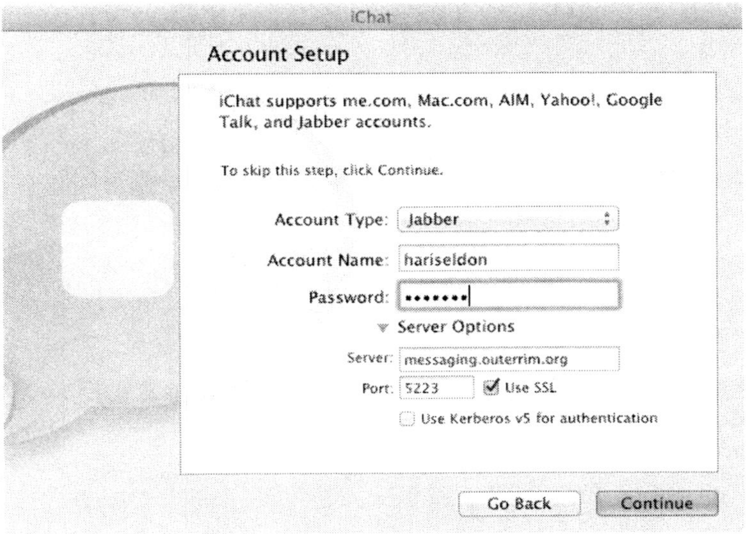

Figure 4-9. Setting up iChat for iChat Server

Conclusion

Once upon a time, people expected mail to allow them to send messages to each other. But today, with Microsoft Exchange, Gmail/Google Apps, and Lotus Notes, most users expect a comprehensive mail solution to also provide shared calendars, contacts, and even instant messaging.

As this chapter has shown, OS X Lion Server is able to do all three. The configuration is simple, but the features provided using the server tools are pretty limited compared to many of the other solutions available with other vendors. But those features aren't always needed. And if they are, many can be enabled from the command line, using the configuration files of the backend services that make up iCal, Address Book, and iChat Server (all of which are capable of running on an iPhone, a Mac, or even a Windows computer).

Productivity isn't just all about groupware though. Now that we've looked at these tools, with obvious productivity benefits, in Chapter 5 we're going to turn our attention to one of the most complicated services in OS X Server that has been simplified about as much as possible. The web service, which also includes blogs and wikis, can be one of the easiest or one of the hardest services to work with, according to what you want it to do!

Wikis, Webs, and Blogs

Lion's web service is open source at its finest. Based on Apache, one of the most popular web engines of all time, the service can host the most complicated of web sites, while being so easy to use that you can start it up by clicking an ON button. The tricky part (and the reason this chapter isn't just one paragraph) is getting the web service to configure wikis and blogs, to run multiple websites on one server, to get specific mods running, and of course, to do all of this securely.

Apache got its name from being "a patchy" product. Many of the aspects of the web that we interact with on a daily basis are made from these patches, known as mods (short for modules). Mods can be enabled or disabled as needed, with each not only providing additional functionality but also providing security concerns and potentially enabling features you may not want (or need).

In this chapter, we'll look at setting up websites, configuring wikis and blogs, and other tasks common in Lion Server environments. We won't dive too heavily into customizing the Apache configuration outside of the options exposed in the GUI, although there are countless things you can do using the Apache, PHP, and other configuration options, such as clustering, securing PHP, enabling options for Perl, and of course, setting up various Ruby on Rails options.

Setting Up a Website

The first step to setting up any web server is to enable the service, which sets up the initial web portal. Before setting up the first website, first complete the items in the Next Steps drawer in Server (see Chapter 2 for more information on completing these steps). These will let you set up the network, users, and most importantly—if you're interested in securely communicating with your server (which most people should be) —setting up SSL certificates.

To create your first website (based on the built-in web portal), open the Server application and click on the Web service, listed under the SERVICES section of the Server sidebar. Here, check the "Enable PHP web applications" if using a PHP-based website.

Click the ON button and when the server is finished writing the settings, a green button will appear beside the Web entry in the sidebar (Figure 5-1).

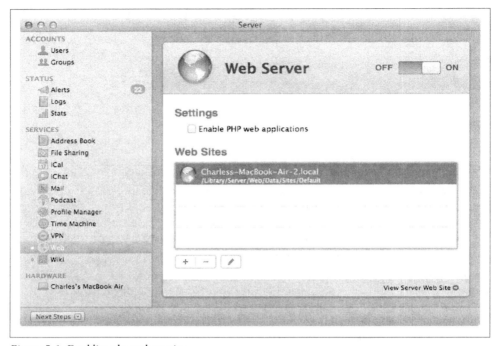

Figure 5-1. Enabling the web service

When the Web service starts, click on View Server Web Site. The default portal should then open, providing you access to Lion's built-in web portal. Here, you can access podcasts, calendars, wikis, and other features, provided they have been enabled.

Accessing the Web Portal

The built-in web portal is accessible using any address that can access the web server that does not otherwise have an address defined. This can be the IP address of the server, the name, or even 127.0.0.1, the loopback address that can be used to access any server from itself. We'll dive further into defining additional websites in the next section. But if all you are using the built-in web server for is the Lion Server portal, then it should be easily accessible at this time.

From the Web service in the Server application, click on View Server Web Site to bring up the portal, or from another server, use the address (name or IP address) of the server to bring up the portal. If you are using a self-signed certificate then you will be prompted to accept the certificate the first time you open the site from another computer. Accept the certificate and the portal will load.

If the portal loads, you'll then be greeted by the Welcome to Mac OS X Lion Server page. Here, links to Mail, Calendar, Change Password, and Profile Manager are included. Each of these links (with the exception of Change Password) requires corresponding services to be configured. The Change Password option is enabled by checking the "Allow users to change their password" box in the site definition screen in Server. The Mail, Calendar, and Profile Manager services are covered in Chapters 4, 6, and 8, respectively.

Uploading Your Own Site

The web portal will change considerably if the wiki service is enabled. The wiki service is covered more fully in the Setting up a Wiki section later in this chapter. The default site uses the */Library/Server/Web/Data/Sites/Default* directory on the server to store files that comprise the website. Once started, copy the files that comprise your website into this directory if you wish to replace the default web portal with your own site. If you do, the calendar and other options are still available, using the address of the site followed by the link for the service. For example, Profile Manager is accessible following the address of the site with /profilemanager, calendars are accessible using /webcal, and mail is accessible using /webmail.

For environments with only one site, if the site loads after copying it to the correct location, the task is often complete. The most important aspect of securing the site though, is locking down the permissions for the files that make up the site. Work with your web developer to make sure the least possible permissions are applied to these files.

Setting Up More Sites

Lion Server is capable of hosting a custom site or the default web portal. As you've seen so far, setting up a website is an easy task. Setting up additional sites is also a fairly straightforward process. When using multiple sites, Apache is pretty smart about how it directs traffic to each. If the address that is used matches a specific URL that is defined in the web service, traffic for that site will go to that location. Additionally, when setting up sites, it is possible to indicate IP addresses that sites listen on, allowing sites to only run on specific IP addresses or ports.

Double-clicking on this site brings up the following options:

IP Address
> The IP address that the site listens on (Any means the site is accessible from any IP address the server is configured to use).

Port
> By default, sites without SSL run on port 80 on all network interfaces, and sites with SSL run on port 443 on all network interfaces. Use the Port field to use custom ports (e.g., 8080).

Store Site Files In

The directory that the files that comprise the website are stored in. These can be placed into the correct directory using file shares or copying using the Finder. Click on the drop-down menu and then select Other to browse to the directory files are stored in.

Who Can Access

By default Anyone (all users, including unauthenticated guests) can access the contents of sites. Clicking on Anyone and then Customize... brings up the "Restrict access to the following folders to a chosen group" screen, where you can choose web directories and then define groups of users who can access the contents.

Allow users to change their passwords

Enables the change password option in the built-in Lion web portal.

View document root contents

A button that opens a Finder screen showing the contents of the root of each web directory.

 If you customize ports to nonstandard ports, many corporate firewalls will block traffic coming to the sites.

Once all of the appropriate fields are filled in, click on Done to save the new site. Then, point the DNS for the domain whose website will be stored on the server to the server. Most DNS hosts have different means of repointing DNS. Usually the root record (e.g., krypted.com) and the www record (e.g., www.krypted.com) both need to point to a server's IP address in order for all users to access the site properly.

Setting Up a Wiki

A wiki is a web page that users create and edit collaboratively. The wiki server in Lion Server can be used to provide a centralized, guided means of accessing content on a server. For example, a teacher may allow students to upload assignments to a wiki, a company may use a wiki to house standard operating procedures, or a family may use a wiki to collaborate on their next daunting trip to the grocery store.

The best-known example of a wiki is Wikipedia, where global collaborators have built and continue to expand on what amounts to probably the largest and most comprehensive repository of encyclopedia-style knowledge. Articles are indexed, searchable, and freely editable from anywhere in the world. While most wikis aren't quite as prolific, I certainly hope that yours will be equally as successful, whatever task you assign to it.

To start using Lion Server's Wiki service, first turn it on. Assuming you are already using the web server, open the Server application to do so. From Server, click on the

Wiki service, listed in the SERVICES section of the Server sidebar. Then, click on the field for "Wikis can be created by." Here, there are two options: "all users" and "only some users." The "all users" option allows any user of the server to create a new wiki article.

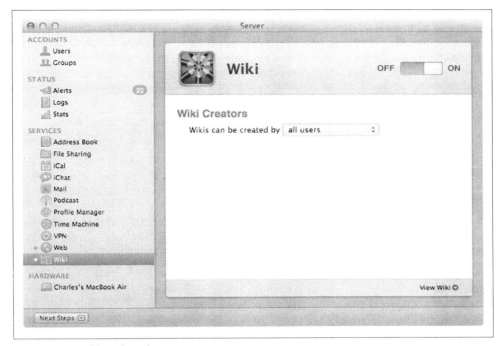

Figure 5-2. Enabling the wikis

Once you have selected the appropriate settings for who can create a wiki, click the ON button. The Wiki server will then start. Once started, click on the View Wiki link to bring up Lion's wiki portal.

Deciding on a Structure

Once the wiki services have been configured and started, it is time to start laying out how people will interact with the wiki. A wiki is a repository. Each page is considered an article of the main repository. Pages can be linked to one another, but do not have to be. No main index of articles is automatically stored, although there are a number of ways to find and link content together. Such a random layout to data puts the onus on the wiki creators and administrators to bring some kind of structure to the environment.

Each topic should have its own wiki, and with each wiki, there can be several ways to lay data out for users to interact with the wiki. One of the easiest structures is to set up a single page that acts as an index to other pages. Another structure would be to have guided lesson plans, where each page links to the next in sequence, much like a *Choose Your Own Adventure* book. There are about as many strategies to take when deciding how the pages will link to one another. The most important thing is to think it through ahead of time.

When there are a lot of pages (exactly how many "a lot" is being up to you), then lay pages out ahead of time graphically. For such a task, consider a tool like Omni-Graffle (*http://www.omnigroup.com/products/omnigraffle*). OmniGraffle allows you to insert pages as, let's say, boxes. Each box can then have arrows that point to other boxes that are in fact pages. Given that many are graphically inclined, this allows everyone to be on the same page quickly and effectively with how pages will link to one another. Many also give users the ability to edit certain wiki articles and therefore will color code each box that represents a page with whether the page is editable by users.

The previous example of a bunch of pages linked from an index page is common in an environment where standard operating procedures are stored in a wiki. Other layouts might include a lesson plan, where an outline may suffice as a map to get to pages from the main page. Another layout might be similar to that used by Wikipedia, where each page only links to items from other pages and with enough total pages, all are linked to one another. A final layout that can be a bit difficult to maintain is a mesh, wherein every page links to every other page.

Finally, when laying out the wiki, take into account that the sidebar will show links to users as well. These include Updates (pages that have been updated since last viewed) and recent documents (the few pages most recently updated). We'll discuss leveraging these further in the section "Accessing Content" on page 98.

Creating a Wiki

To create your first wiki, open the Lion Server web portal by entering the server's address (name or IP address) into a web browser (assuming no custom URL or port must be used to access the site). At the first screen (the home page if you will), click on the link for Wikis, bringing up the URL for the site followed by /wiki/projects. For example, if the site is *https://wiki.krypted.com*, the full path to the wiki would be *https://wiki.krypted.com/wiki/projects*.

At the Wikis page, the bar at the top is used to navigate through content. The button to the far left of the bar opens a ribbon in the center of the screen reminiscent of MobileMe accounts, giving the options to navigate to the items on the home page. The Wikis link to the immediate right of use the ribbon takes users to the list of wikis, with individual wikis listed underneath (if you have navigated into them) and articles within wikis listed under that. To the right side of the screen are actions, including a search box (reminiscent of Spotlight) used to search content, the lock icon used to authenticate or log out of the wiki, the cogwheel, used to delete wikis and access settings and the plus sign to create wikis.

Click on the plus sign and a menu appears giving the option to create a New Wiki as well as create wikis and documents within My Documents. My Documents are private and for this example we will create a wiki that is accessible to a group. Click on New Wiki to do so.

The Create a new wiki screen then opens. Provide a name and description for the wiki in the appropriate fields (try to use as many keywords as possible in the description field to increase the likelihood that users can find relevant content). You can also use the Upload image... button in the Wiki Icon section to define a badge, or icon, that is displayed when opening the wiki. Click on the Next button to then define who has access to the wiki (Figure 5-3). Here, add all users that will need access to the wiki, similar to how permissions are handled with regards to file sharing (covered further in Chapter 3).

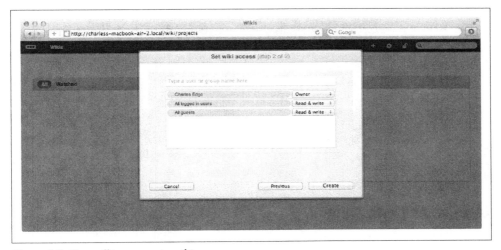

Figure 5-3. Controlling access to wikis

 When defining permissions, the "All guests" entry includes users who have not entered a username and password, whereas the "All logged in users" covers users who have authenticated, no matter the groups they are or are not in.

Once comfortable with the permissions settings, click on Create to create the new wiki. The Setup Complete screen is then displayed with a button to Go to Wiki. Click on the button to enter into the newly created wiki.

At this point, the first wiki page is displayed. The navigation bar at the top of the screen shows a new icon (a pencil). Clicking on the pencil changes the bar to a WYSIWYG editor, which can be seen in Figure 5-4. Here, the icons (from left to right) allow you to attach a file, embed an image, embed an audio or video clip, insert a table, embed

HTML (yes, even YouTube embeds), choose styles for text, select formatting for text, insert links (useful for keeping pages you create connected to one another), justify text within a page, insert bulleted lists, and indent content. To the far right of this screen, click on Save to commit any changes you make and click on Cancel to undo any changes.

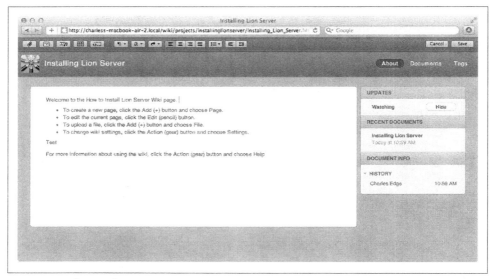

Figure 5-4. Editing wikis

Collaborating with Others

According to their permissions, some pages can only be edited by single users. Others can be edited by a lot of different people. It can then become difficult to identify who changed certain parts of pages (and why) in topologies where multiple users are contributing content. To provide a little sanity here, each change and the user who made each change is tracked in the DOCUMENT INFO sidebar. Here, each update is shown, along with the time the update was made and the user who made the update. Clicking through each will show old versions of pages as well as a button to Show Changes, which highlights changes and shows deleted items with a strike-through. The Restore button can then be used to revert to a saved version of the page if content was inappropriately changed (Figure 5-5).

Having a transparent history of who changed each aspect of the system then strengthens the argument for collaboration. Being able to revert to old versions means that more people can change content, allowing for more content contributors.

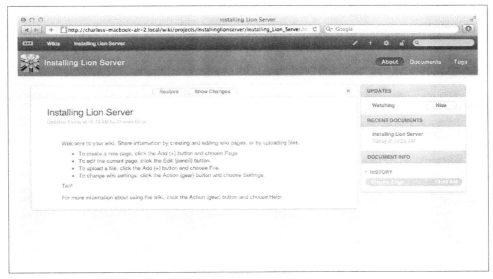

Figure 5-5. Wiki versioning

Customizing the Wiki

Wikis are dynamic content that is user generated. But because the wiki service is integrated with other parts of the server, if you are running calendars and blogs, content from those services can also be dynamically loaded into the wiki. To insert blocks (similar to blocks in Moodle, or Widgets in WordPress), to the righthand sidebar of the wiki, go to the wiki settings (using the cogwheel icon in the navigation bar at the top of the screen) and then click on Services for checkboxes to enable Calendar and Blog integration.

You can also customize the look and feel of the pages that are loaded. Apple is known for its beautiful design, so it's hard to second-guess them on these things.

Customizing the look and feel of the wiki server is one of those things people will do less in Lion Server than in previous versions of OS X Server. Gone are the big banners that say "Mac OS X Server" and footers that rub in what operating system the wiki is running on. Apple no longer includes a dozen or so templates to choose from. Instead, it's a single, highly integrated and functional collaboration server portal.

But you can still customize the look and feel if you want to. Graphics files are stored in */usr/share/collabd/coreclient/public/stylesheets/cc/img*. While most graphics are stored here, not all elements are. For example, a common task might be replacing the login picture icon with that of a school's mascot by replacing the */usr/share/collabd/ webauthd/public/images/user.png* image with an image of your own. To add a custom banner or edit the look and feel, edit the *.css* files stored in the */usr/share/collabd/coreclient/public/stylesheets/cc*. For example, to change the color of text, use the color setting in the body section of the *core.css* file. Or change the background color of unused space using the background-color setting of the main section.

Blogs

Blogs are a stream of consciousness. My blog (*http://www.krypted.com*) now has around 2,000 posts, and other than the occasional link between articles to build on topics, it's just a reverse chronology of technical exploits and the occasional banter about football or some other random topic. Blogs aren't usually meant to guide users to content. Instead, they're meant to simply be user-generated content. Blog articles can certainly be referenced in wikis, where a wiki guides users to content.

Blog articles can also dynamically appear in a wiki. Blog articles are not meant to be collaborative. Once an article is published, it's meant to stay fairly static. Multiple users do not have access to edit one another's blog entries. Before creating entries though, first to set up the first user blog.

Creating a User Blog

Each user in a Lion Server environment can have a blog. The ability to enable and use the blog is then up to each user. To enable a user's blog, open the My Page site that is listed on the main site. Once open, click on the cogwheel icon to bring up a menu and click on Settings.

At the Settings page, click on Services. At the Services screen, click the checkbox to enable the user blog and then click on the Save button to create the site.

An entry in the Settings sidebar then appears. Click on Blog to see options for defining who can access the blog. Type the name of a user or group in the provided field. Then select the level of permissions that the users or groups selected should have (read only, read and write, or no access). The two entries already provided are by default given no access. If you want anyone in the world to see the blog, change the "All guests" entry to "Read Only" (Figure 5-6). If you want only users with accounts on the server (e.g., the members of your family, students or staff at your school, etc.) to have access, leave "All guests" set to "No access" and change "All logged in users" to "Read Only."

Users can then comment on each blog entry. By default, comments are disabled. However, they can be enabled on a per-blog basis. To do so, set the Comments field to Anyone or Authenticated Users. Once set, click Save if you wish to enable commentary. Also, consider who can moderate comments. For a larger environment, there may be a lot of commentators, whereas for a smaller environment, it may only be a given teacher. Click on Comment Moderation and set it to All Comments.

When you are finished filling in all of the appropriate information, click Save to commit any changes to the system and you will be finished setting up your initial blog.

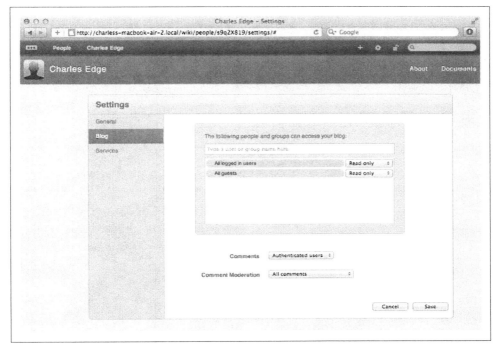

Figure 5-6. Managing blog permissions

Editing the Blog

Each user who has the blog service enabled has a profile and (hopefully) blog entries. To edit the user profile, click on the People option from My Page and then click on the pencil icon in the top row of the screen. This will bring up the same WYSIWYG editor we looked at earlier in the chapter.

From the same screen, click on the plus sign ("+") at the top of the screen and click on New Blog Post in My Blog (Figure 5-7). Editing the blog is similar to editing a wiki. However, when you do so, the content is then accessible in reference to the user. Clicking on People at the home screen shows each user.

Under the Settings entry for each user, the icon for users can be changed to custom art files (e.g., a photo of the user).

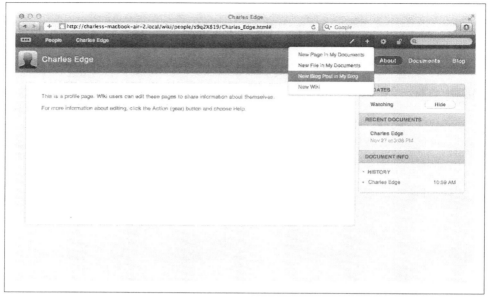

Figure 5-7. Accessing a user's blog

Accessing Content

When an organization allows anyone to create content, the sheer volume of content can make it difficult to find any content when someone needs it. The more content, the harder it is to wade through it all. Apple has provided a few tools just for such issues.

The first is Spotlight integration with web services. From any screen in the web portal, click on the hourglass field and begin typing text until a match comes up. Click on the selected match for the search and you will be taken to the page for that entry. This is one of the most simple features to use, but also one of the most powerful.

Another way to guide visitors to relevant content is to have them visit the appropriate page. From the main page that acts as a gateway into the portal, click on My Page to see updates to your content. For example, if someone has commented on one of your articles, then you will see the new icon, indicating new content that you should be aware of. A list of users can be directly accessed using *https://127.0.0.1/wiki/people* and then clicking on each will show you their specific page.

The Updates option from the main portal page casts an even wider net. Here, click on the Showing field. As you can see in Figure 5-8, you can show only items you've marked as favorites, only your own content, items that have been marked hot by others, or all items.

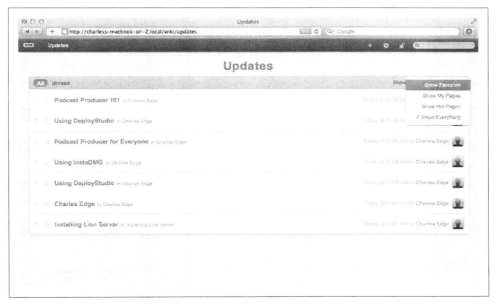

Figure 5-8. Using favorites

For many, constricting the output of various searches is a critical aspect of finding relevant content. For others, it is not a very important aspect of managing web services. A common entity it might not be great for is someone that doesn't really use many services other than redirecting other websites.

Site Redirection

Redirection is taking traffic for a given website and redirecting that traffic to another. In this example, we'll place this index page in the web directory for *http://www.krypted.com* on an OS X Lion server. The server runs a site for *https://www.krypted.com* already and so this page is simply meant to redirect users to the https version of the site:

```
<!DOCTYPE HTML PUBLIC "-//W3C//DTD HTML 4.0 Transitional//EN">
<HTML>
<HEAD>
<TITLE>krypted.com Secure Redirect</title>
<meta http-equiv="REFRESH"
content="0;url=https://www.krypted.com">
</HEAD>
<BODY>
You will now be redirected to https://www.krypted.com
</BODY>
</HTML>
```

Above, we create an HTML tag, a heading tag, a title tag, and finally the meta http-equiv refresh. The content used between the body tag is simply to inform a user who might happen to see this site what is happening. Simply copy this into an HTML file and you're off to the races. If using OS X Server, you can drop into */Library/WebServer/ Documents* by default to redirect users elsewhere.

Conclusion

In this chapter, we have looked at a lot of different aspects of the OS X Web server. Lion server is a great Apache server, capable of serving up large, extremely complex and powerful sites. Apache can be clustered in ways that allow administrators to scale servers up into environments. So that mini Server you may be running can scale with you if you so choose.

We also looked at the more common sites people tend to use these days. This includes the internal wiki and blog services that OS X server is capable of providing. While we looked at editing minor graphical elements, with the wiki and blog services, most are going to simply stick with what Apple has designed on our behalf. After all, they're probably known for design more than we are.

Now that we have a functional web server, we can build other functional or media intensive tools into the playground. In Chapter 6, we will take a look at a service that is easy to manage but complicated due to spam: Mail.

Building a Mail Server

Mail is one of the easiest aspects of Mac OS X Server to manage. Managing all of the things that go into protecting a mail server, on the other hand, can be one of the more challenging aspects of managing a mail server on Mac OS X. Lion Server has many features that help to protect your mail server; however, spammers and virus writers make their living off of the distribution of their nasty little wares. Therefore, managing a mail server is a constant battle to keep up-to-date on the latest trends of mail serving, to keep your server able to communicate with other mail servers on the Internet.

Before You Install

Before you sit down to install your own Lion Server as a mail server, think carefully about what you are about to do. If you only have a few accounts, then a solution like Hosted Exchange (*http://www.microsoft.com/exchange/en-us/exchange-online-hosted-email.aspx*) or Google Apps (*http://www.google.com/apps*) might be a better fit for you. This isn't because managing the Lion Server is difficult; it's not. But the ecosystem that goes into mail can be frustrating.

If you do decide to continue, there are a few tasks to perform before you get started. These include getting a domain name (e.g., krypted.com), configuring the DNS for that domain name (e.g., mail.krypted.com), configuring the IP address you use through your Internet service provider (ISP), and making sure that the IP address the ISP gives you isn't blacklisted.

Registering a Domain Name

Most organizations already own a domain name. Most also already have a website for the domain name and potentially a host of other services. But not all do. And certainly, it's easiest to set up a fresh, new domain when setting up a mail server. To set up a domain, first go to one of the bevy of registrars or companies who sell domains. These include companies like Network Solutions, Go Daddy, Register.com, and hundreds of other companies that can sell domains. I usually like to leave DNS on the registrar.

Finding the right domain name can be tricky. Take into account how it will look on business cards, how you will spell and say the domain name on phone calls, and how closely it resembles how you will use the domain name. For example, if you clean carpets and your name is Bill, then chances are you wouldn't want johnspipes.com.

Configuring DNS

Once you have a domain name, it is important to know which DNS servers are used for the domain. You can use Network Utility to query the domain name and you should get back a list of DNS servers. If DNS is hosted by the registrar, then there will usually be a control panel to log in and make changes to the DNS records that comprise the name. When considering DNS, there are two issues to take into account. The first is that you should have an A record (for more on records, zones, and other DNS fun, check out Chapter 9) that points to mail.domain.com. For example, for krypted.com, you would want a record that points to mail.krypted.com.

Mail isn't the only DNS record to make. If you have separate DNS servers for POP or IMAP and SMTP, then you can also have separate records for each service (e.g., imap.krypted.com or smtp.krypted.com). In addition, you will also want a record that points the MX record to the name of the server.

Reverse DNS

In addition to A records and MX records, reverse DNS records (or PTR records) are important as well. Many spam prevention solutions require the PTR record match the forward lookup record (which is usually an A record or a CNAME). The authoritative DNS server for the IP address is going to be your registrar. Therefore, the registrar should be able to create such a record for you.

Because you will need reverse DNS, it is highly unlikely that you will want to use a dynamic IP address as the public address of your mail server. If you do, few domains will accept your mail. Overall, this represents a few steps so far. First, obtain a domain name. Then build the correct records on the DNS service and finally contact the ISP to verify that you have a static IP address and that a PTR record has been created for the IP address that the server uses on the ISP's DNS servers. This provides the best chance that the IP address being used will be allowed to relay outgoing mail as needed.

Making Sure the IP Isn't Blacklisted

Something else to consider about the public IP address used for your mail server is that it hasn't been blocked by one of the spam blacklists. Even if you have all of the previous requirements, if the IP was blacklisted before it was given to your organization, then you may have some work to get the address removed from blacklists. A great site for checking the blacklists is *http://whatismyipaddress.com/blacklist-check*.

From the Blacklist Check site, locate the Blacklist Check field and enter the IP address of the server. Then click on the Blacklist Check button and the IP will be checked against each blacklist database. The green checkmarks mean the server isn't listed (Figure 6-1).

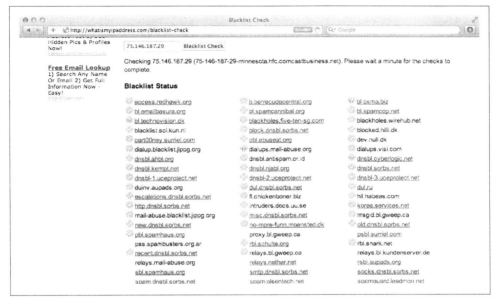

Figure 6-1. Checking for blacklistings

If the server is listed on any of the blacklists, then contact each of the blacklisting entities individually to have the issue resolved (once the server is not an open relay, used for routing spam, etc.).

Installing the Mail Service

Many of the tasks to perform before configuring the mail service are out of your control, making it frustrating. Now for the easy part. To set up the mail service is one of the easier tasks to perform in Lion Server. One reason being that Lion Server comes with a Service Configuration Assistant that will configure the server as needed. First, enable the Mail service.

Enabling Services

To enable the mail service, open Server Admin and click on the name of the server in the Server Admin sidebar. Then click on Settings in the Server Admin toolbar (horizontally at the top of the Server Admin window) and click on the Services tab. Click on the checkbox for the Mail service and then click on Save.

The Mail service will appear under the name of the server. Click on the service and then click on the Overview button in the Server Admin toolbar. Click on the Configure Mail Service... button to bring up the Service Configuration Assistant for the mail service, which will guide you through the setup of a mail server.

At the Introduction screen, a list of technologies that comprise the Mail service is shown (e.g., Postfix, Dovecot, Kerberos, Mailman, etc.). Click on Continue to proceed to the Mail Service: General screen. Here, use the first three checkboxes to enable each protocol used in your environment. These include the following:

POP (Post Office Protocol)
Downloads messages to your computer, usually removing them from the server immediately or after a certain number of days

IMAP (Internet Message Access Protocol)
Leaves messages on the server so that all mail clients stay in synchronization with one another (including Mac OS X, iOS, and Windows clients)

SMTP (Simple Mail Transfer Protocol)
The protocol used to send mail through a mail server and used to route mail between mail servers

For most modern environments, IMAP and SMTP will be all that is required. Provided the mail server will be used to accept mail, also configure the following options (as shown in Figure 6-2):

Allow incoming mail
Enables incoming email on the server (via SMTP)

Domain name
The name that the server will listen to mail for (e.g., for an address that is cedge@krypted.com, the domain would be krypted.com)

Host name
The name of the server (e.g., mail.krypted.com)

Hold outgoing mail
Holds outgoing mail for approval

Relay outgoing mail through host
If your ISP allows you to relay outgoing mail through them or if you have a third-party service that filters outgoing mail, enter it here

Once you are satisfied with your options, click on the Continue button.

At the Mail Service: Filters screen are options to check mail for spam and viruses (Figure 6-3). The options for each are as follows:

Scan email for junk mail
Enables Spam Assassin as a junk mail filter for the full server (almost always use this feature if you're not already)

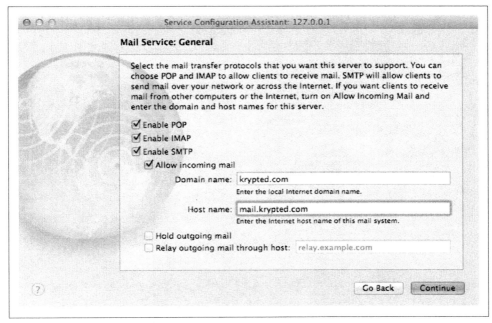

Figure 6-2. *Configuring mail services*

Minimum junk mail score
> Used to configure how aggressively the junk mail filter will work (the default setting, which is 6, is a good start, although you can always increase or decrease later if you encounter false positives)

Scan email for viruses
> Enables the ClamAV virus scanner on incoming mail

Infected messages should be
> Choose whether messages that are flagged as having a virus are deleted, bounced (or sent back to the user from whom the message originated), or redirected (sent to a special mailbox for infected email)

Update the virus databases
> Number of times per day (evenly distributed throughout the day) that the ClamAV virus scanner updates itself from the ClamAV repository

Click on the Continue button, once the options are appropriate for your needs. You will then be looking at a bunch of checkboxes on the Mail Service: Security screen (Figure 6-4). Here, you are simply choosing which protocols the mail server will use. By default, these are secure (requiring SSL certificates). Unless you need to add POP access, leave them as they are, as any protocol not enabled during the setup assistant can be enabled once complete.

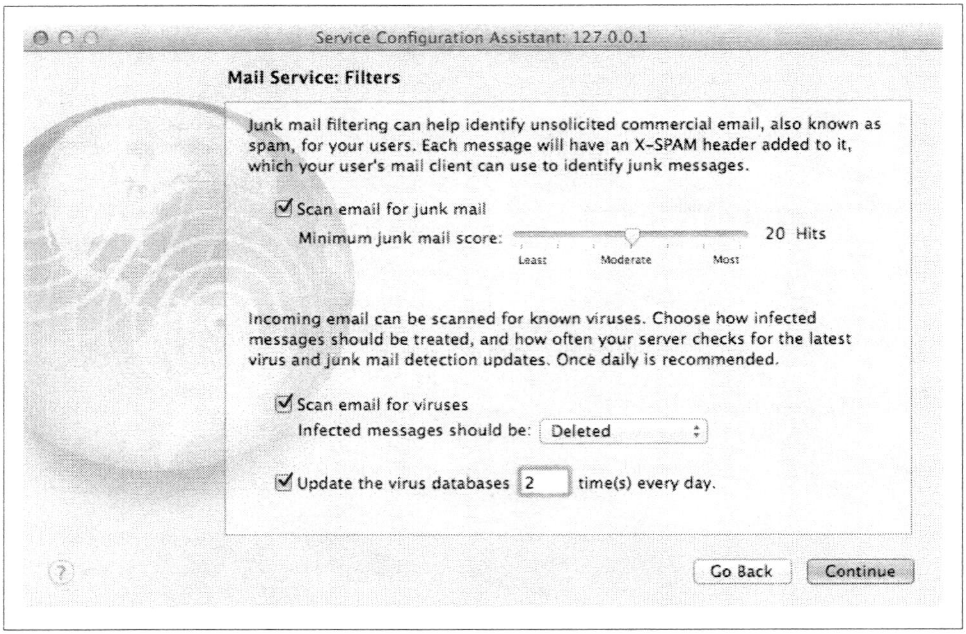

Figure 6-3. Configuring message protection

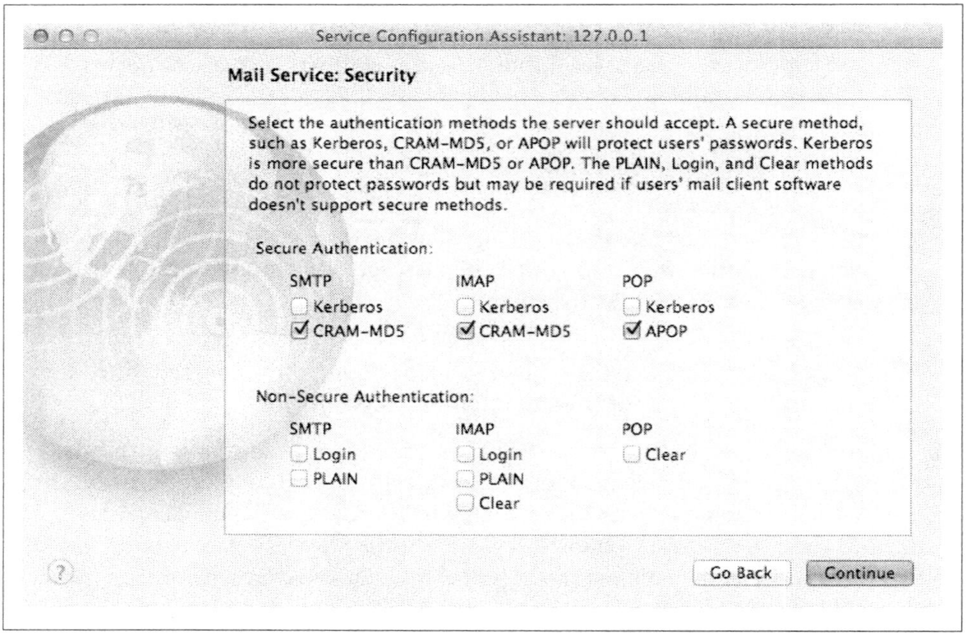

Figure 6-4. Enabling protocols

Click on the Continue button and you will be taken to the Mail Service: Mail Storage screen. The default location of the mail store (or the directory that all of the email is stored in) is */Library/Server/Mail/Data/mail*, as you can see in Figure 6-5. If you will be using an external storage array, such as a Thunderbolt drive, then you can choose to use a mail folder stored there by unchecking the "Use default mail store location" box and then using the Choose button to locate the desired alternative location. Additionally, the Local Host Aliases section at the bottom of the screen can be used to add additional names to the mail server (e.g., if you use a name other than those listed to access the mail server).

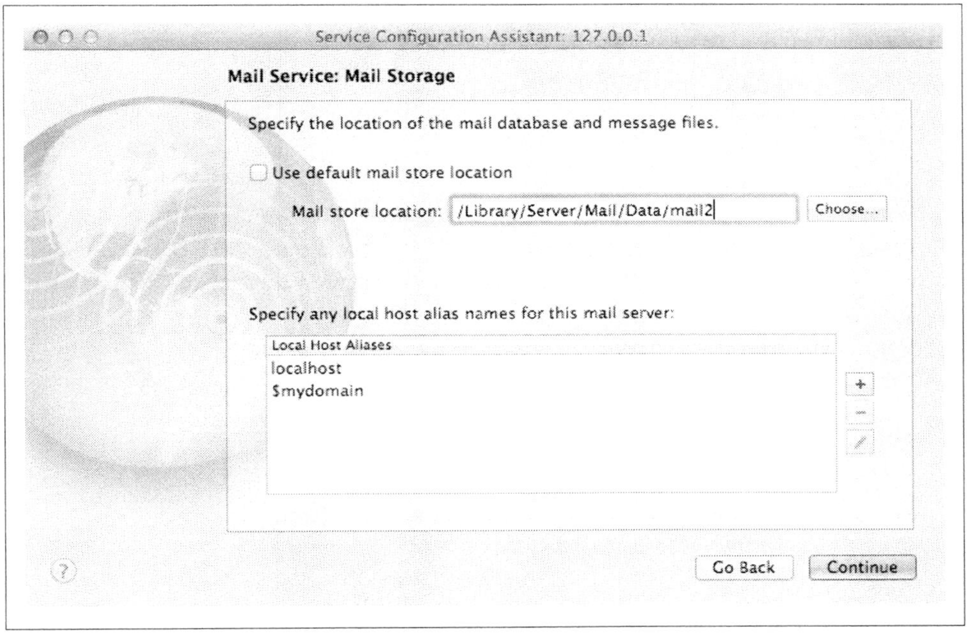

Figure 6-5. Setting the path to the database

Click on the Continue button and then review the settings that will be used at the Mail Service: Confirm Setup screen. If they are as intended, click on the Continue button to finish setting up your mail server.

Configuring Options

Once the assistant has completed, the services are configured. You can then more finely tune each service from Server Admin if you need anything that wasn't configured by the Assistant. This might be mailbox quotas, who can relay (or send) mail through the server, mailing lists, and various degrees of what gets logged. A common feature to enable that isn't covered in the service configuration assistant is mail quotas.

To enable mail quotas, open the Server Admin application from */Applications/Server* and click on the Mail service in the Server Admin sidebar. Then click on the Settings icon in the Server Admin toolbar (which runs along the top of the window) and click on the Quotas tab. Here, you will see a number of settings (seen in Figure 6-6) that include the following:

Refuse messages larger than
>Sets the maximum size of a mail message that the server will receive, configured in megabytes (e.g., 1,024 megabytes being 1 gigabyte)

Enable quota warnings
>Enables a warning that gets emailed to users who are close to their quota; this is also known as a soft quota

Send quota warnings when usage exceeds
>Sets the percentage of the quota that triggers an email to a user that they are nearing their message limit

Edit Quota Warning Message
>Customizes the message sent to users who are almost over their quota

Disable a user's incoming mail when they exceed 100% of quota
>Also called a hard quota, this setting disables mail for a user when their quota has been exceeded

Edit Over Quota Error Message
>Customizes the message sent to users who are over their quota

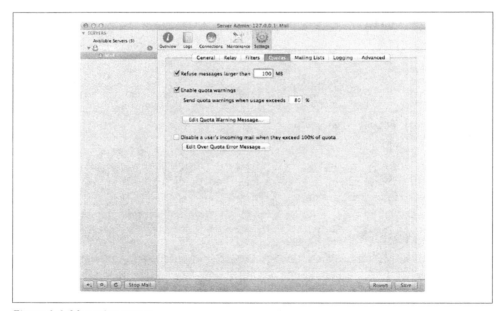

Figure 6-6. Managing quotas

Quotas are then configured per user in the Workgroup Manager application (covered in Chapter 2). The Mail tab provides an option for setting the quota for each user. As many environments have a lot of users, you can use the Command key to select multiple users and set their quotas concurrently.

The configuration options in Lion Server also include automatically clustering the mail service. This is pretty cool for really large environments, as you can add multiple mail servers to the cluster as environments grow. Such a feature is only required in very large environments, and even with the sleek assistant to leverage when clustering, administrators still need a fairly advanced knowledge of managing large scale messaging environments to fully implement the functionality.

Configuring Users

Once the mail server has been set up, you will need to create email accounts. Email accounts can be created in the Server Application or using Workgroup Manager. To create an account, open the Server application (e.g., by using LaunchPad) and click on Users in the ACCOUNTS section of the Server sidebar. Then click on the plus sign ("+") to bring up the New User window. At the New User screen, provide the following information:

Name
    The name of the user, as it should appear to people receiving mail
Address
    The user's email address
Description
    A simple description of what the account is used for (e.g., work email)
Incoming Mail Server
    The IMAP or POP server being used
Outgoing Mail Server
    The SMTP server being used

Click on Done to create the new user account. The user will then have the email address provided in the Email Address field, provided that the domain used in the email address (e.g., oreilly.com) matches a domain local to the mail server.

Installing Clients

The mail server isn't going to be very useful unless you configure a client to access the services it hosts. The two main platforms that Lion Server is built to host mail for are iOS-based devices (e.g., iPad and iPhone) and Mac OS X clients (e.g., MacBook Air and MacBook Pro). The protocols that are hosted by the mail server are standards-compliant and are accessible by any platform, provided that platform supports IMAP and POP, both of which are standards compliant mail protocols. In this chapter, we are just looking at Apple devices as clients, but the settings we use for those are also usable on other platforms (and with other mail clients) as well. We will also be looking at using IMAP for both devices. If you will not be keeping mail on the server and wish to use POP instead, then interchanging the IMAP settings for POP settings is a fairly straightforward process.

Setting up iOS Clients

Configuring the mail client in iOS to work with a Mac OS X Server can be done manually or by using a configuration profile. Configuration profiles are covered more fully in Chapter 9, so here we will focus on manually configuring an iOS device to work with a Lion-based mail server. To get started, open the Settings app and then tap on the Mail, Contacts, Calendars setting in the Settings sidebar. From the Mail, Contacts, Calendars, Settings tap on the option to Add Account... (as seen in Figure 6-7).

At the Add Account... screen, you will be shown a number of options. Tap on Other.

The Other screen has buttons for adding mail, LDAP, CardDAV, and CalDAV accounts. Tap Add Account... (Figure 6-8).

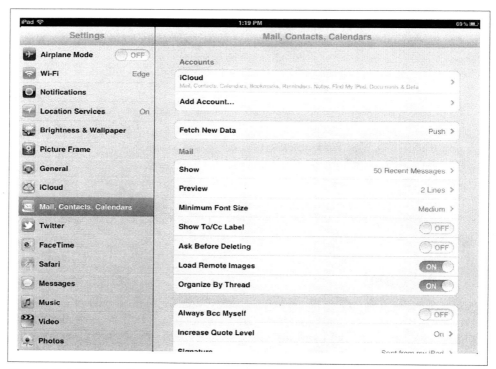

Figure 6-7. Adding a mail account

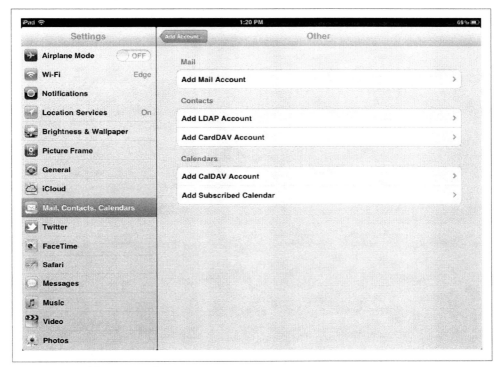

Figure 6-8. Enabling just mail

Enter the name of the user (as it will appear to people they send mail to), the address (which is the email address for the user), the password (which is the user's email password entered into the Server application when the account was created) and a description (which is a note about what the account is used for), and then tap on the Next button. Chances are that the server will not allow automatic configuration of the account on the iPad. Here, you can choose between POP and IMAP accounts (as referenced earlier, we're using IMAP). The New Account prompt would then require the following settings (seen in Figure 6-9):

Name
    The name of the user, as it should appear to people receiving mail

Address
    The user's email address

Description
    A simple description of what the account is used for (e.g., work email)

Incoming Mail Server
    The IMAP or POP server being used

Outgoing Mail Server
   The SMTP server being used

Figure 6-9. Mail server settings

When providing names for the mail server, make sure that you have taken into account whether the name will resolve properly whether inside the network or logging in remotely. Also, many networks block SMTP, so it is never a bad idea to have users log into the VPN in order to send mail, which allows SMTP traffic even if the other network blocks such traffic (as the data is sent through the VPN tunnel).

Tap on the Next button once the settings are entered and the account will be set up. The user can then use the Mail app on the iOS device to send and receive mail through the server.

 There are settings for granularly configuring how the iOS device handles mail. These are found in the Settings app under Mail, Contacts, Calendars.

Configuring Lion Mail Clients

Configuring the IMAP client in Lion is very similar to doing so on an iOS-based device. Open Mail and then click on the Mail menu and select Preferences... to bring up the Mail Preferences screen. Then click on Accounts and click on the plus sign ("+"). The Add Account window appears. Here, provide the full name (the name that will appear in mail sent from the user), the email address (the email address of the user being configured as provided in the Server app when the account was created), and the password.

If an email autodiscover record has been created in DNS, then the account will automatically be configured. Because few domains still use these records, you will more than likely be prompted for the Incoming Mail Server screen. Here, provide the following information (as seen in Figure 6-10):

Account Type
Select IMAP from the drop-down menu (unless you wish to use POP)

Description
A short description about what the account is to be used for

Incoming Mail Server
The IP address or DNS name of the email server

User Name
The account name as provided earlier in this chapter

Password
The password for the user's account

Figure 6-10. Configuring account details

Click on the Continue button once the appropriate settings are provided and then the Incoming Mail Security screen comes up. Here, you want to use SSL if possible to keep the communications with the server as secure as possible. Click on Continue to bring up the Outgoing Mail Server screen. Here, provide a description in the Description field, the IP address or DNS name of the server in the Address field, the account name in the User Name field, and the user's password from the Server application in the Password field, as seen in Figure 6-11.

Click on the Continue button and at the Outgoing Mail Security screen, check the box for SSL if you have a certificate available on the outgoing mail server (which is likely the same as the incoming mail server for most smaller environments). Click on Continue again and then at the Account Summary screen, check that the settings shown match those from the server, and then click the Create button. The new account will then synchronize with the mail server and if you can send and receive mail for the account, you have finished the setup process.

Figure 6-11. Configuring outgoing mail

Leveraging Push Notifications

Traditional clients to servers pull information from the server. If an email is sitting on the server then the email will get synchronized on a time interval. But mobile devices (for which power consumption is critical), require a new way to interact with servers. Push notifications are different in that the mobile device doesn't perform a pull on the server, but instead is notified by the server that there is something for the mobile device to access only when there is something new.

Setting up push with email in iOS 5 with Lion Server couldn't be easier. To do so, open the previously configured mail account using the Mail, Contacts, Calendars option in the Settings app. Then, tap on the Fetch New Data button to bring up the Fetch New Data screen. Here, set the Push setting to On, as in Figure 6-12.

Once enabled, you will see a badge when new mail is available. In the Notification Center, accessible using the Notifications option in the Settings app, you will also have the option to more granularly configure where the notifications appear and how, as you can see in Figure 6-13.

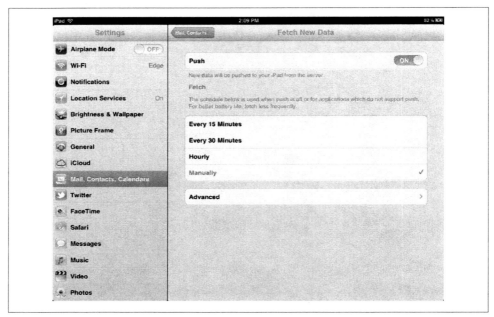

Figure 6-12. Enabling push

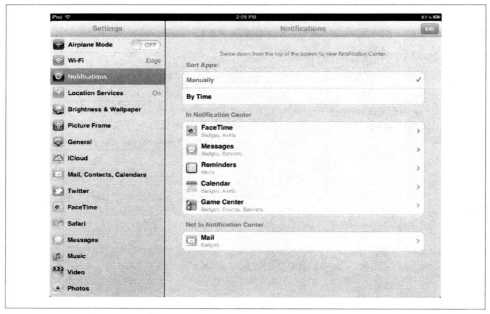

Figure 6-13. Configuring notifications

Protecting Mail: Message Hygiene

Spam, viruses, and other junk is the part of managing a mail server that just plain sucks. There is so much junk out there that mail has to be treated far different than any other service. Special precautions need to be taken to reduce junk mail both within the server and before the junk mail gets to the server. Doing so will keep the server running optimally and keep the message queue from getting bogged down attempting to process mail that should have never been queued in the first place.

Spam Filtering via MX Records

One of the best ways to filter out spam and viruses is to just use a third-party service to do so. You can still enable various spam filters on the server itself (and you should). However, a third-party service will block out much of the junk mail before it comes into your network, freeing up your server to be far more effective in the tasks you actually want it to perform.

Most of the third-party spam filtration tools work by intercepting mail before it comes to your server and then delivering filtered mail to the server. These can operate in one of two ways. The first is as an add-on for your firewall, or gateway, appliance. Cisco, SonicWALL, Barracuda, and many others build solutions for these types of uses (you can easily build your own filter using SpamAssassin and put it in the demilitarized zone of your network, if you have one). The second way to filter mail before it gets to the server is to use a third-party service. Examples of these include Postini (now a part of Google and soon to be called Google Message Continuity) and McAfee SaaS Email Protection (formerly called MXLogic).

Reducing incoming traffic to the network will likely stop at least one major network or mail server outage. This might be from a massive accumulation of spam that is being scanned by SpamAssassin, by a large quantity of viruses hitting the server at once, or just the wide area network connection to your network going down. Wait, did I forget to mention the best part of the services? They queue up mail if your mail server goes offline and allow you to change IP addresses on the fly to deliver mail to a backup mail server, if need be.

Clam Up Viruses and Send Assassins After Spam

Filtering spam and viruses before they come to your server is a great idea. But not everyone can do so, and even for those who can, the server should still run a local instance of a spam and a virus filter. As you likely noticed while running the setup assistant, both of these are built into Lion Server. These include ClamAV, the anti-virus tool, and SpamAssassin, the spam filtering tool.

Once the server is set up and configured, there are a few things that are important to know about ClamAV and SpamAssassin. The first is access to global configurations for both through Server Admin. The second is that while we are only going to look at the tools in Server Admin, there are also a lot of command-line options and options in configuration files that can be used to customize the server. A good reference for SpamAssassin is *http://www.amazon.com/SpamAssassin-Alan-Schwartz-PH-D/dp/0596007078/ref=sr_1_1?ie=UTF8&qid=1322104074&sr=8-1*. ClamAV is well documented online.

Access the options in Server Admin by clicking on the Mail service and then clicking on Settings in the Server Admin toolbar. Click on Filters to bring up the virus and junk mail filters. Here, you can set the languages that the server will accept mail from, add information into the subject line (useful for setting up client rules that take this tag into account), notify recipients of mail that a virus was found, and set the frequency the virus database is updated (7 is a good minimum value for this).

You can also set the junk mail score. SpamAssassin rates the likelihood an email is junk by assigning numerical hits to certain rules the message violates; for example, if a message has the word Viagra in it, the number of hits will likely increase by one. The slider at the top of the Filters shows the minimum score before a message is treated as junk, as can be seen in Figure 6-14.

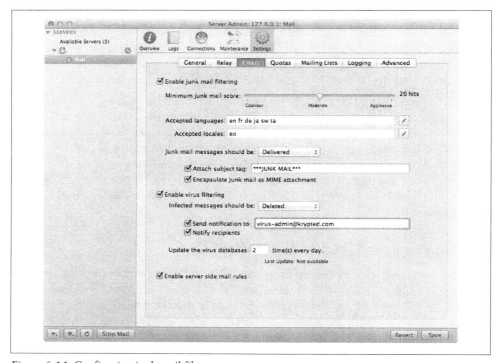

Figure 6-14. Configuring junk mail filters

If you are relying on using the spam and virus filters in Lion Server, I recommend at least using a subject tag or bouncing junk mail outright. I also recommend bouncing email that has been infected by a virus. Either of these can cause problems in certain circumstances. If the server gets a lot of messages that need to get sent back to the sender, then those messages can clog the queue. If this happens, disable the filters temporarily (or set the messages to be deleted).

Configuring WebMail

Once you are confident that the server is well protected and set up properly, it is time to use WebMail. WebMail is great for when users are not in front of a computer owned by the organization. WebMail is built on the open source RoundCube project, and when configured appropriately, accessible from anywhere in the world. WebMail is automatically configured when the web service is started. For more information on the web service, see Chapter 5.

The actual setup of the web service can be oversimplified as being: Open the Server application (from */Applications*), click on Web, and click the ON button (Figure 6-15).

Figure 6-15. Enabling the web service

Once On, click on the Mail service and check the box for Enable WebMail (Figure 6-16).

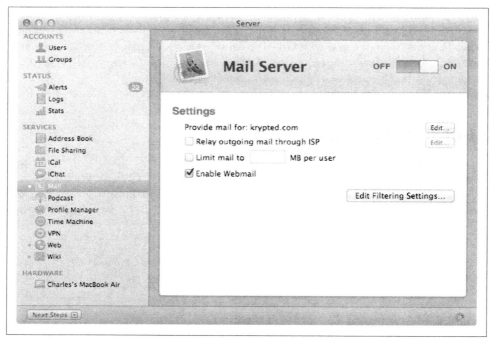

Figure 6-16. Enabling WebMail

 WebMail can take a few minutes to start. Do not try to access the site until the progress indicator in the bottom right corner of the screen stops.

Using WebMail

Once enabled, WebMail can be accessed from the Welcome to Mac OS X Lion Server page, shown by visiting the name or IP address of the server's default website, by default. Each site that is created can be suffixed with /webmail to access WebMail for all users. For example, if the server is called mail.krypted.com, then use https://mail.krypted.com/webmail to access WebMail.

 Alternatively, you can use the Welcome to Mac OS X Lion Server screen and click on Mail to access WebMail.

When accessing WebMail, you are initially met with a login screen. Provide a username and password for the server that has email enabled.

Don't use the user's email address as the username, use the short name entered when the account was created. Once you log in as a user, you will see a screen somewhat similar to the Mail application in Lion (Figure 6-17). From here you can compose messages, read mail, sort mail into folders, and search through your existing mail. The search feature in Lion can search within attachments, an option new in Lion Server.

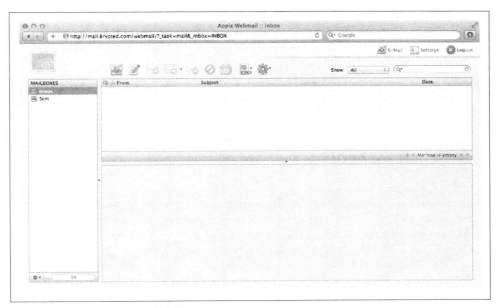

Figure 6-17. Logging into WebMail

Additionally, you can set up server-side rules (provided they were enabled in the Filters screen of Server Admin). Here, you can set up rules to handle messages that are above or below a specific size, have a specific recipient (e.g., a lot of mailing lists use the recipient as the address of the list), have a specific sender (the person sending you the message), or have a specific item in the subject line of the message. The subject line is a great place to configure rules to manage spam (e.g., move spam into a folder called Spam), as can be seen in Figure 6-18.

Figure 6-18. Using server-side rules

You can also compact a mailbox (or defragment the mailbox). For users who are close to exceeding their mail quota, the compact feature can help recoup any lost space. To use the compact feature, click on the cogwheel icon below the MAILBOXES list in the sidebar. Then, click on Compact as seen in Figure 6-19.

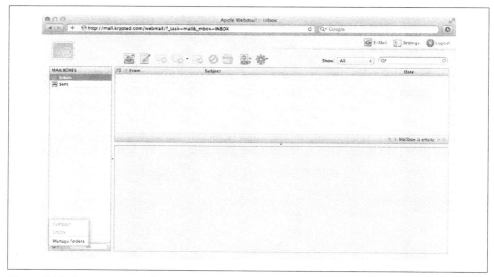

Figure 6-19. Compacting mailboxes

Finally, for further information on managing the WebMail service in Lion Server, hover over each icon to bring up a tool tip with a description of what the button does.

Conclusion

Apple's servers have been doing mail since long before the advent of Mac OS X. Over the years, the mail services get more and more mature with each passing revision. While built on solid foundations, the mail service is a breeze to configure and the long-term care and feeding of the services should be minimal. However, before you deploy a Lion mail server, first make sure that all of the steps we laid out first are performed. These included making sure the DNS was set up properly, configuring the web service (if you will be using WebMail), setting up users and hopefully filtering mail before it gets to the server using one of the options provided earlier in this chapter.

The backend of each service is open source, meaning that thousands of servers around the world use the same technologies that Apple uses in Lion Server. These include RoundCube, SpamAssassin, ClamAV, Postfix, Amavis, and Dovecot. But you don't need to know how to manage each of these individually. Instead, you can use Server Admin to maintain the mail service, which combines all of these in one easy to use interface.

Now that we've covered most of the standard services that are common to many server platforms, we'll turn our attention in Chapter 7 to a service that is interesting and very functional for anyone looking to create video content and unique in Lion Server: Podcast Producer.

Building Your Own Podcasting Server

A podcast is a file containing video and/or audio that people view over a network connection. Podcast Producer is Apple's solution for recording, distributing, and accessing podcasts. Podcast Producer can be linked to iTunes, allowing users a one-stop shop for accessing rich media. Often used in schools and corporate training, Podcast Producer is one of the more elegant solutions for podcasting, using tools built into Mac OS X to make it easier than ever to capture video (which includes screen captures and audio-only podcasts) and distribute the content to users.

While Podcast Producer makes it easier than ever to work with video, it is one of the more complicated services built into Mac OS X Server. Leveraging directory services, web services, grid computing and often mass storage, Podcast Producer has a lot of moving parts. If any part isn't firing properly, then the whole solution will not function.

There are two ways to set up Podcast Producer. The first is a simple workflow where all podcasts are posted to a website. Once posted, podcasts can be viewed on the website, the feed can be aggregated using RSS (we'll look a bit more at RSS later in this chapter), or the podcast can be subscribed to and viewed from within iTunes. The second setup for Podcast Producer has all the same options, but comes with few by default. This is a more manual configuration, but allows you to do practically anything you desire (e.g.,, watermarking content, merging clips with introductory videos, or layering Keynote presentations or additional audio tracks to the workflow).

Given that little has changed with the second setup since Snow Leopard and that our focus here is on ease of use, we will focus on the first style of configuration in this chapter. Using Podcast Producer in this fashion, you can be up and running in minutes, hosting your own podcast and sharing it with friends via iTunes.

This style of Podcast Producer works by using a client application, Podcast Publisher, to create these rich media files. Once created, the files are uploaded to the server for processing. The processing can include simple items, such as watermarking a file (or putting a logo in each frame of a video file), adding scenes to the front and back of a file to show information about the file (e.g., title, copyright, and author), and publishing to a site or RSS feed. Apple makes all this seem easy, but it's actually pretty difficult to do under the hood (which luckily we don't need to know anything about).

Before You Begin

Before you get started with Podcast Producer, there are a few things to take care of. In this example, we will use a standard implementation of Podcast Producer. The tool is capable of much more, but we will focus on getting your server up and running so you can extend what it does at a later time. Podcast Producer has a number of prerequisites though. These include web services, DNS, Directory Services, IP addresses, and ports to forward (if the podcast will be accessible from outside of the network).

The IP address of the server should be static. This is true for most services, but dynamic IP addresses (e.g., DHCP) on a Podcast Producer server will cause the services within the server to become unresponsive. Not only will podcasts be inaccessible because users are looking at the wrong IP address for them, but in addition, the service will fail to function, even if you repoint users at a different IP address. DNS and the hostnames that make up a properly resolvable server are important for the same reason. These two are covered thoroughly in Chapters 1 and 2, so if you have any problems with them, go back and review those chapters.

Each Podcast Producer will need to run a shared directory service, such as Open Directory. The directory service is important, but if you do not yet have a functioning Open Directory, you will be prompted to set one up during the deployment of Podcast Producer. This eases the deployment of Podcast Producer and ensures you will have functional usernames and passwords to access content, create content, and authenticate Podcast Producer services to one another.

The Podcast Producer server will need to be running the web services. The web services supply the portal that users visit to see published podcasts. For more information on enabling the web service and configuring a site, see Chapter 5. If the server will be accessible outside of your network, then ports must be opened on the firewall. For more on the web service portion of Podcast Producer, also see Chapter 5. In addition to the web services, though, the ports 8170 and 8171 will need to be opened for the Podcast Capture and podcast command-line tools, if those are to connect to the server remotely.

Building Podcast Producer

Once you've completed all of the prerequisites, it is time to set up Podcast Producer. To make setting up Podcast Producer as easy as possible, Apple has included it in the Server tool. To install Podcast Producer, open Server (from /Applications) and click on the Podcast entry in the Server sidebar. Here, click the ON button to enable the service.

Once enabled, choose who can view the Podcast library (the site that hosts the podcasts, which we will cover later in this chapter) by choosing Anyone, Authenticated Users, or

Podcast Owners from the Settings drop-down menu. Anyone includes users without passwords, whereas Authenticated Users only allows users that have a username and password access to each podcast's feed. Podcast Owners further restricts access to each podcast to the owner of the podcast by default. We will look at assigning more granular permissions to podcasts later in this chapter, but for now we will assume that all Authenticated Users have access to podcasts, but only users who have passwords to authenticate into our directory service.

Additionally, you will want to see Podcast Producer in Server Admin. To do so, open Server Admin and click on the name of the server. Click on Settings in the Server Admin toolbar and then click on the Services tab. Click on the checkbox for Podcast Producer and then click on the Save button, which places the Podcast Producer service in the Server Admin sidebar under the name of the server, as seen in Figure 7-1.

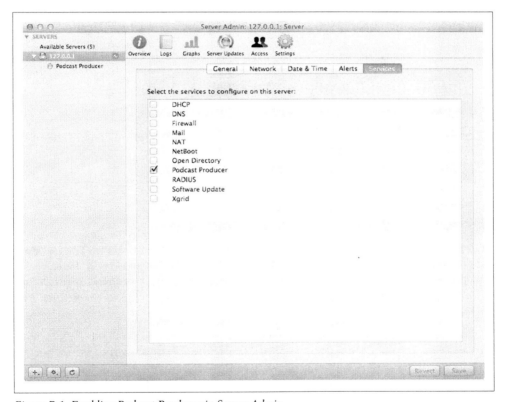

Figure 7-1. Enabling Podcast Producer in Server Admin

Once configured, let's look at capturing our first podcast.

Podcasting

There are a number of books on how to make great podcasts. They mostly involve the content and the format of the podcast. Few involve the technical implications of podcasting. Here, we're not going to look at much regarding how to make a good podcast. Instead, we'll give a few more technical tips and then quickly move on to making your first podcast:

- Do not have an introduction clip for each episode that is longer than the body of the episode. This tends to bug people as they watch each episode.
- The better the camera, the better the podcast will look. For testing things out, the built-in camera on Apple computers is a great tool to use. However, for long term podcasting, consider getting a nice camera (especially if you end up with a lot of viewers).
- Define the audience. Think about who will be watching your podcasts. This helps you speak more directly to the desired target audience.
- Use an outline. Just like writing a paper, first start with an outline. Define what you want to say and how you want to say it. You can go so far as to build an entire script, just try not to make it look overly rehearsed if you're reading a script.
- Rehearse. When you make podcasts in Podcast Producer, you can try over and over until you get it just right. Watching yourself speak, listening to your own inflections, and watching yourself follow along with your outline will help immensely.
- Have fun. People like to see others having fun. So feel free to throw out all of the previous bullets if they keep you from doing what is most important: enjoying yourself.

Making Your First Podcast with Podcast Publisher

Podcast Producer is the server software that you will publish podcasts to. Podcast Publisher is the application that runs on Mac OS X Lion clients that you will use to create the actual content. To use Podcast Publisher, open it from *Applications/Utilities*. Once open, click on the New Podcast button in the lower-right corner of the screen (Figure 7-2).

A corkboard-looking screen will then appear. At a screen similar to Figure 7-3, provide a name for the Podcast in the top section. This name will be shown to visitors of the web portal, so choose something relevant to the content you will be creating. Each episode of the podcast is shown as a sticky on the corkboard. Click on Add a new episode... to create your first episode.

Figure 7-2. Making a new podcast

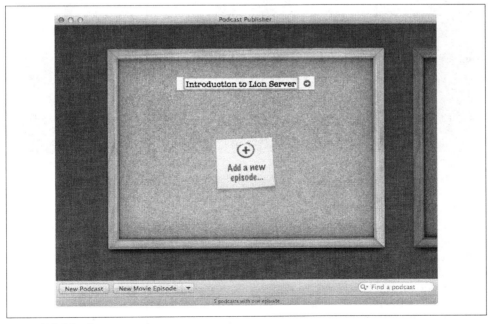

Figure 7-3. Naming your podcast

The screen will then show you video, as displayed by your camera. You can record episodes as a screen capture instead, if you so choose. To switch to the screen capture screen, click on the button to the right in the lower-left corner of the Podcast Publisher screen (Figure 7-4). Whether recording a screen capture or a video from the camera, click on the red button to initiate a three-second countdown to begin recording.

 Sound is displayed below the video. Try to keep audio levels to the middle of the bar. Audio is shown as green, yellow, and red. If the audio goes into the red, then viewers will likely experience poor audio quality.

Figure 7-4. Podcasting with screen captures

After the countdown, video will begin recording. Click on the button again to stop the recording. If you are doing a podcast that includes the screen on your computer, during the countdown is a good time to minimize the Podcast Publisher screen. Otherwise, the screen is shown in the podcasts. Once the podcast is recorded, use the yellow bar at the bottom of the screen to trim any footage from the beginning or end of the video (e.g., the part of the video where you opened Podcast Publisher again and stopped the recording). Once the video is recorded, click Done to save it to the corkboard, or use the Share button to publish it (Figure 7-5).

Figure 7-5. Sharing your podcast

If you are sharing the podcast, you can save it to the following (each of these use the name of the episode as the name of the new file):

iTunes
> Saves a copy of the movie in the Movies section of iTunes

Mail
> Opens a new email and saves a copy of the movie in the email as a QuickTime movie (*.mov*)

Desktop
> Saves a copy of the movie in QuickTime (*.mov*) format on the desktop of the currently logged in user

Podcast Library
> Saves a copy for viewing in the web portal (covered in the next section of this chapter)

Remote Workflow
Uses a Custom Workflow to process the video or audio

For this example, share the video to the Podcast Library (Figure 7-6).

Figure 7-6. Sharing videos to the Podcast Library

That's it. You've now published your first podcast. Next, we'll look at viewing what you have published!

Accessing Content

Why capture a podcast if no one can view what you're working on? All published podcasts are kept in the Podcast Library. This library is viewed from the built-in web portal installed with Lion Server when you enable the web service.

Viewing Content

To access a podcast episode, open the default web portal installed in Lion Server. Then, click on the Podcasts icon.

At the Podcasts window, you will see all of the podcasts that you have access to (Figure 7-7). Each user will, by default, own podcasts they create. If the permissions for new podcasts was set to Podcast Owners, then other users will, by default, not see each others podcasts. If you uploaded podcasts but do not see any, click on the lock icon, and when prompted, authenticate with the same credentials used to create your first podcast.

Figure 7-7. Viewing a podcast

Click on the name of the podcast to access the podcast's screen, shown in Figure 7-8. Here, you can see each episode of the podcast (previously you would have seen them on the corkboard). Click on the Play button to view each episode of the podcast.

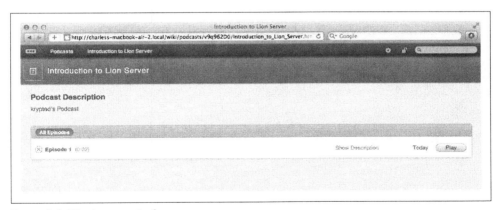

Figure 7-8. Viewing an episode

Podcasts are displayed using a QuickLook screen. Here, click on the X or press the Escape key to close each podcast's screen.

Restricting Access to Podcasts

At any point, you can change the permissions for each podcast. This means you can set podcasts (not episodes of podcasts, but podcasts themselves) up in such a way that only specific users and/or groups can access content.

To limit who can access a podcast, browse to a specific podcast and then click on the cogwheel icon in the grey bar at the top of the screen. Click on Settings to bring up the permissions screen, shown in Figure 7-9. In the box below the field "The following people and groups can access this podcast," enter the short name of a user or group who you would like to allow access to a podcast. Users and groups that match the search string you enter will appear. Click on the appropriate entry and the user or group is listed in the list below the field. Here, click on the drop-down list of permissions options to set what kind of access the user or group has to the podcast.

Each user can have "Read only" or "Read & write access." If a user is not listed, then they are inherently not able to access the podcast. Users and groups with "Read only" can watch podcasts while users and groups with "Read & write" can edit the podcast using the Podcast Publisher utility described earlier in this chapter.

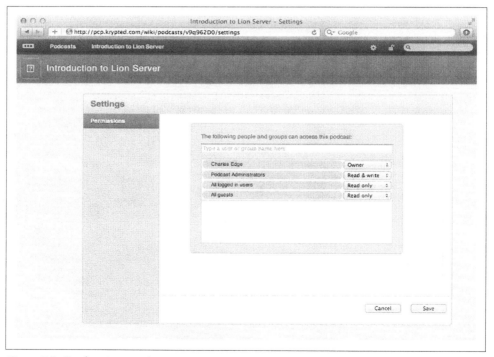

Figure 7-9. Configuring a podcast's permissions

Once all of the users and groups you want to access a podcast are appropriately configured, click on the Save button and then test viewing a podcast while logged in as a user who was just configured (or a user who resides in the appropriate group).

Connecting with iTunes

Content is accessible through a web interface. But using that web interface, you cannot watch content when not online. iTunes is Apple's default media player, available on Windows and Mac OS X. Given the popularity of the client, Apple uses it as an aggregator for Podcast Producer-based content. This is known as subscribing to a podcast. When subscribed to a podcast from Podcast Producer, iTunes downloads and caches each podcast that is published automatically. Podcasts can then be viewed from an airplane, on the road, or using fleets of laptops in class, with little fuss.

To subscribe to a podcast using iTunes, first open a podcast. Then, click on the cogwheel icon and click on Subscribe in iTunes....

iTunes then opens and shows the podcast caching (Figure 7-10). Accessing podcasts from then on out involves simply opening iTunes and clicking on the Podcasts icon in the iTunes sidebar. From here, all podcasts that are downloaded will be shown.

 Blue dots beside the name of a podcast episode indicate whether or not an episode has been watched. This allows viewers to quickly discern which episodes they have seen versus which episodes they haven't.

When we are setting up servers for the first time, we often test features. It is easy to imagine that the first few tries at podcasting will result in limited success. Therefore, to delete a podcast, simply control-click (or right-click if you have two buttons on your mouse) on the name of a podcast and click on Delete to remove the podcast from within iTunes.

Customizing Workflows

As mentioned at the beginning of this chapter, Podcast Producer is a very complicated service. You might be wondering why it didn't seem so complicated so far. The reason is that Apple has made an extremely vanilla version of Podcast Producer that is configured when using the Server application in conjunction with the Podcast Publisher tool. But you can do much, much more. Some of these additional features include watermarking, adding titles, merging videos, extracting audio, and distributed rendering to help push some of the processing power of moving all those pixels around to other computers.

Figure 7-10. Viewing episodes in iTunes

 The same prerequisites apply to Podcast Producer when set up in this fashion that pertained to Podcast Producer when set up using the easier method earlier.

To get started, we're going to perform a new installation of Podcast Producer. Because we added the service to the Server Admin sidebar earlier in this chapter, we can now access Podcast Producer by clicking on its icon from within Server Admin. Once open, click on the Configure Podcast Producer... icon in the lower-right corner of the screen.

At the Podcast Producer Setup Assistant, click on Continue at the Introduction screen and the assistant will read the Podcast Producer settings. At the Express or Standard screen, click on Express Setup and then click on the Continue button.

At the Directory screen, click on Continue (if you aren't yet running Open Directory, you will be prompted to configure a new Open Directory Master). At the Confirm screen, you will then see each setting that will be configured. Note that by default, NFS and Xgrid are configured, which handle storage and rendering respectively.

Creating Workflows with Podcast Composer

Once Podcast Producer has been reconfigured, podcast workflows are created using the Podcast Composer tool. Podcast workflows are automations that apply to the podcasts that allow you to assign all of the cool features that made you want to use the more complicated rendition in the first place. To get started, open Podcast Composer (installed in */Applications/Server* when you install the Server Admin Tools) and you will see a string of tasks, or stages.

The first stage is Information. Here, provide the name of the workflow, a name for the Author (note this does not need to match a username, so the author can be something like "O'Reilly Authors"). Also provide a description, such as "capture a single source of input, watermark it, add titles, and publish to the Wiki." Once you've got the Information set as you want it, click on the Import stage.

At the Import stage, select where the content will come from when submitting to the workflow. This can be Single Source (one QuickTime movie), Dual Source (two Quick-Time movies) or Montage (documents accessible from QuickLook). For the purposes of this example, hover over the Single Source and click on the icon in the lower-right corner of the image to expand the pop-up and select Single Source type (Figure 7-11). Here, click on Audio Device Only, Screen Recorder Only, Video Device Only or leave set to Any for the workflow to select any type of media (which is what we will do in this example). Click Done and then click on the Edit stage.

At the Edit stage, you will by default see four tasks, as indicated in Figure 7-12. From left to right these are the introduction video, the title screen, the body, and the closing animation, known as the Exit movie. Hovering over the I icon (short for information) allows you to select more information about each. For example, there are multiple Introduction movies, or you can browse to include a custom movie for both the Introduction and Exit movies.

 Click on any of these and then press the Delete key to remove that task from the Edit stage.

In this example, we will only change the watermark. To do so, click on the Information icon for the third task and then set the Watermark field to the Apple logo. Then click on the Export stage. Here, you can set what formats, or codecs, that Podcast Producer will render video with. By default, video is set to H.264, the most common standard on the web today. We can leave it as is, and then click on the Publish stage. By default, new videos are only published to the Library.

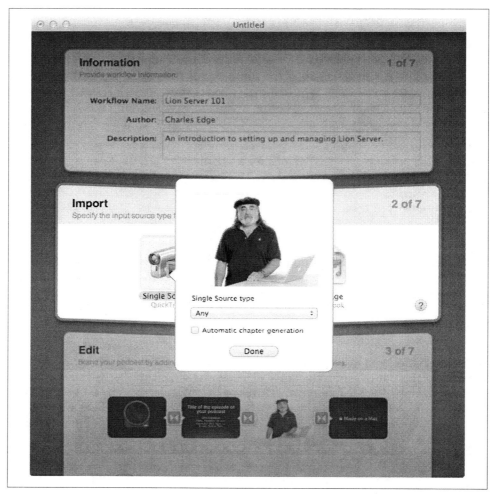

Figure 7-11. Choosing a type of podcast

In this example, we'll post our movies to a Wiki page (see Chapter 5 for more information on Wikis). Click on the plus sign to add the task and select Wiki from the menu. At the Wiki popup menu (Figure 7-13), provide the name of the server as well as a username and password to post content to the wiki. You can select blogs or wikis as destinations, but for the purpose of this example, we'll leave the default setting as the Submitting user's blog (selecting custom blog or wiki requires a user or group name for the object, respectively). Also, click on the Library item and provide the credentials and address for the server.

At the Notify stage, you can select various methods of notification, such as using iChat or emails to let users know that a new podcast episode is available. For this example,

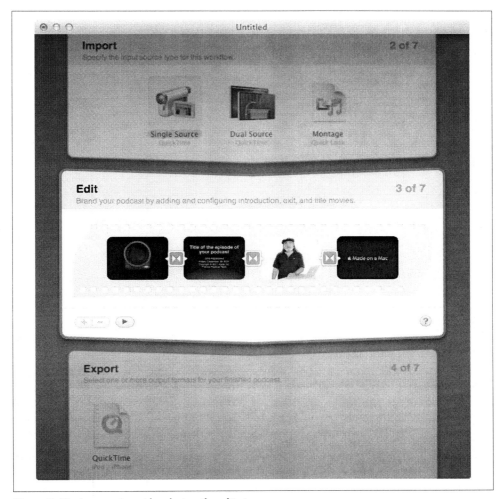

Figure 7-12. Automating video during the edit stage

we won't be using any notifications, so click on the Summary stage and then click on the Save button to save the workflow to a file on your computer or Deploy to push the workflow to the Podcast Producer server. Click on Deploy to bring up the Server dialog box. Here, provide the address of the server and if asked, provide a username and password in the Name and Password fields respectively to publish the new workflow to the server.

 If Kerberos is working from the client that the workflow is being created on, you will not be prompted for a name and password.

Figure 7-13. Publishing to a wiki

Securing Workflows

Workflows have usernames and passwords saved within them. These are not accessible from clients, but they might provide access that is not desirable in the wrong hands. Additionally, some workflows are made for certain individuals or groups (e.g., a Math 101 workflow for the teacher of the Math 101 class shouldn't be accessible to the teacher of the Art 101 class). Therefore, you can lock down who can access each workflow.

When you deploy a workflow to a server, it can be seen from within Server Admin (located in */Applications/Server* by default). To secure a workflow, open Server Admin and click on the Podcast Producer service in the Server Admin sidebar. Click on the Workflows icon and then click on a workflow that you would like to secure. By default, each workflow allows access to all users and groups with accounts on the server (so guests cannot publish podcasts, but any user with an account can). Click on the "Allow access to [Workflow] for the following users and groups" radio button and then use the plus sign to add users or groups to the list that can access each workflow, as seen in Figure 7-14.

There are three workflows that are built into Podcast Producer by default. Rather than deleting these workflows (notice the lack of a Delete button for workflows), you can restrict access to them to an empty list of users.

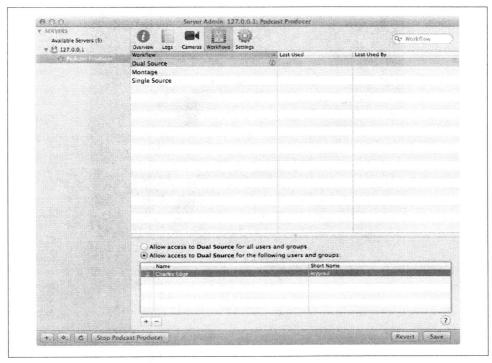

Figure 7-14. Workflow access controls

Podcast Capture

Once workflows are secured, it is time to create some episodes for each. To do so, use the Podcast Capture tool, located in */Applications/Utilities* by default. Podcast Capture is a legacy tool, only for use with custom workflows. When opened, you will be prompted to log in. Click on the Log in button and then provide a username and password that has access to the workflow we created earlier in this chapter. Once authenticated, you will have the ability to select between the following types of inputs, or captures (Figure 7-15):

Video
> Capture content using the camera (built-in or attached)

Dual
> Upload two QuickTime movies

Screen
> Capture movies using a screen capture

Audio
> Capture an audio track using the default sound input of the computer

Figure 7-15. Defining inputs

To access the workflow we created earlier, click on Screen. Then click on the red button to start the recording. Once finished, click on the button again to stop the recording. Rehearsals are important. Therefore, if you'd like a do-over, click on the Start Over button; otherwise, click on the Publish button to bring up the Podcast Information screen (Figure 7-16). Here, provide a name for the episode, a description, and if appropriate, select a custom workflow. The podcast will then get uploaded to the server when you click the Publish button.

Remote Recording

Podcast Producer can also start workflows that capture content from other cameras. These cameras are bound to Podcast Producer and then activated when running Podcast Capture and selecting the bound camera as the input source. This is popular in lecture captures, recording games, and even at my house, trying to steal food (yay for motion sensors). The first step is binding a camera.

To bind a camera to Podcast Producer, open Podcast Capture from the computer from which the camera is to be bound. Click on the Podcast Capture menu at the top of the screen and then click on Preferences to bring up the Podcast Capture preferences screen. Here, click on Audio/Video and you should see the Video Source, Microphone and Quality. Select the video source (in such situations they are normally external cameras),

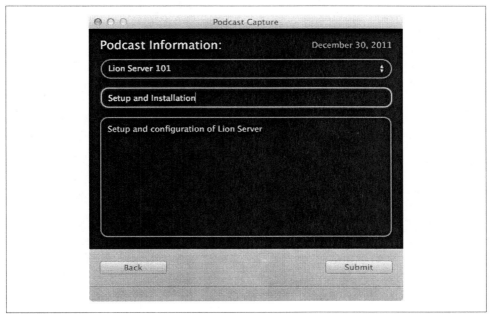

Figure 7-16. Podcast information

the appropriate microphone, and then choose Best from the Quality drop-down menu (the files are not that much larger than they would otherwise be and they look way better). Once the appropriate camera is selected, click on Start Sharing....

When prompted, provide the address and credentials to use in binding the camera. Then, the camera will be listed in Server Admin under Cameras where you limited access to Workflows. Access to cameras can be limited in the same fashion. When starting a Video capture on another computer, you will then have a list of cameras available within the screen. Selecting the bound camera shows the video streaming from that camera.

Conclusion

Podcast Producer is a great solution for quickly and easily posting video or audio to a website. This video can then be aggregated using an RSS feed, websites, or even iTunes. This becomes a great way to keep the family updated on what is going on with the kids, get training videos to your users, or even teach a class of kids how to dissect a frog.

But Podcast Producer is one of the more complicated solutions bundled into Lion Server. The initial installation example shown in this chapter is very basic, with podcasts being made available on a website and in iTunes. Very little automation is done on the video. We are capable of doing much more, as shown in the later sections of the chapter. Using the more complicated features, extremely complicated workflows can be strung together, providing unlimited abilities, once you layer scripting and third-party products on top of these workflows.

Now that we've finished looking at various collaboration services in Lion Server, in Chapter 8 we will turn our attention to using policies to control aspects of client systems. The remainder of the book will then be dedicated to these types of infrastructure-based services.

Managing Apple Computers and iOS Devices

Lion Server has three features used to centrally manage Mac OS X and iOS-based devices. Traditionally, the most common feature used is Managed Preferences, an extension to Open Directory that allows administrators to control settings, or preferences, on Mac OS X-based computers. In Lion, a new feature, called Profile Manager is included.

Profile Manager is the future of managed clients for Mac OS X and iOS-based devices (iPhone, iPad, and iPod Touch). Profile Manager provides an enrollment system for Mobile Device Management, allowing administrators to remotely control settings, such as controlling the dock, locking down application access, and setting up policies for device access. Profile Manager also allows administrators and users to lock or wipe devices in the event they fall outside the control of the organization (e.g., they are lost or stolen).

Additionally, Lion Server includes Software Update Server for Mac OS X clients. Software Update Server is a tool used to cache software updates. Once cached, administrators of Lion Servers can choose which updates to send to client computers. Having a centralized update server can be an extremely useful tool. Not only does the software cache help keep all users running the same version of the operating system, but the shared cache also reduces wasted bandwidth on the organization's Internet connection by hosting updates inside the network.

In this chapter, we will look at each of these, giving administrators of Lion Server powerful tools to streamline the client systems that are in their care. These tools then comprise a considerable part of the client deployment strategy and mobile device management strategy for small and large organizations alike.

Profile Manager

Profile Manager is the latest addition to the features that comprise Mac OS X Server. Once set up and configured, Profile Manager acts as a web portal that gives administrators granular control over devices in their care. Profile Manager can remotely manage Mac OS X and iOS devices, and does so through a web portal that is both easy for administrators to use and available and simplistic enough to provide access to end users as well.

Before you set up Profile Manager, first complete a few basic tasks:

1. Verify Connectivity to the Internet
2. Verify that you have a valid Apple ID (preferably a generic account, as it will be used on the server)
3. Download and install Lion Server (described further in Chapter 2)
4. Configure incoming TCP ports for the server for ports 443, 1640, and 5223 (see Chapter 9 for more information on managing TCP ports on OS X Servers if you are using an OS X Server as a firewall)
5. Either create a self-signed SSL certificate or purchase one from a certificate authority (CA)
6. Verify that the hostname is in alignment with the hostname defined in DNS

Additionally, Profile Manager will need to be connected to a directory service. If the server is not a member of a directory service, such as Apple's Open Directory or Microsoft's Active Directory, then the server will be set up as an Open Directory Master (described further in Chapter 2) during the setup process for Profile Manager.

Once all of the prerequisites are met, to get started with the installation, open the Server application and click on the Profile Manager in the SERVICES section of the Server sidebar. Then, click on the Configure... button at the Profile Manager screen (Figure 8-1).

The Configure Device Management wizard then opens. Click on the Next button to begin configuration. If the server is not running as an Open Directory Master, the Configure Network Users and Groups screen will appear, indicating that the server will be configured to be an Open Directory Master. Click on the Next button to bring up the Directory Administrator screen, where the login information is displayed for the Open Directory Master.

The username is diradmin by default, given that the directory has a different username and password than the local administrative accounts. The username can be changed. Provide a password for the directory administrative account and then click on the Next button.

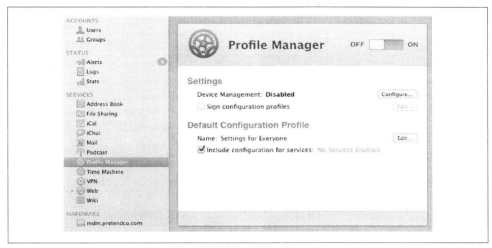

Figure 8-1. Configuring Profile Manager

At the Organization Information screen, provide a name for the organization in the Organization Name field (e.g., O'Reilly) and an email address for the administrator of the domain (preferably a generic address, such as odadmin@companyname.com). Then click on Next and click Set Up at the Confirm Settings screen, provided the Open Directory settings match the desired configuration.

The Open Directory Master will then be set up. If the server is using a self-signed certificate then you will see the Configure an SSL Certificate screen, where the certificate that you configured in Chapter 2 should be selected (Figure 8-2). The name on the certificate should match the hostname of the server. Once the appropriate SSL Certificate is selected, click on the Next button.

At the Get an Apple Push Notification Service certificate screen, provide a valid Apple ID and the correct password for that Apple ID. Click on the "Get certificate" button when you have provided the correct information for the Apple ID (Figure 8-3).

 You do not need to have an Apple Developers account for the Apple ID used with Profile Manager.

The Apple push certificate that enables MDM is then installed (a process that requires the server to connect to the Internet). When the APNS certificate (Apple Push Notification Service) is installed, the server will indicate that your server meets all Profile Manager requirements. Click Finish at this screen and the final settings will be written to the server.

Figure 8-2. Selecting an SSL certificate

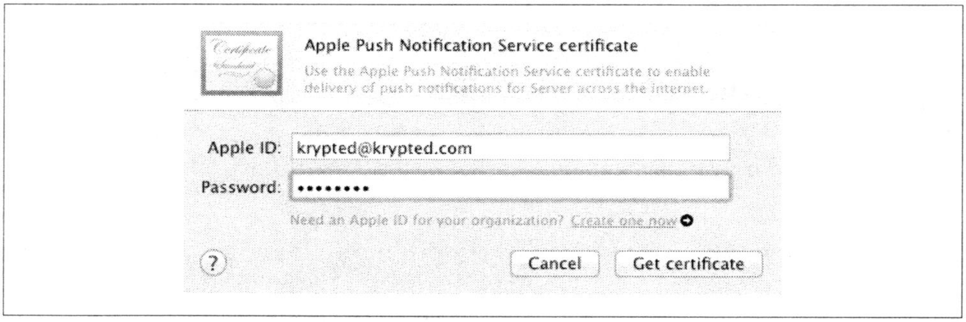

Figure 8-3. Providing an Apple ID

Back at the Profile Manager screen, just click the ON button to start the service and you should then be able to access Profile Manager using the URL of the server followed by /profilemanager. For example, if your server is called *MDM.krypted.com*, then you would access Profile Manager by opening the URL *https://MDM.krypted.com/profile-manager* and authenticating with a user configured to have access to Profile Manager (more information on configuring Service Access Control Lists in Chapter 2).

Setting Up Profiles

Once Profile Manager is enabled, the next step is to actually create profiles. When planning for profile deployment for users, groups, and computers, it is important to consider the order with which profiles are applied in the event of a conflict. Profiles are applied in the following order:

1. User
2. Computer
3. Computer Group
4. Everyone
5. User Group

What this means is that when you apply a profile, if you set a setting for both a user and a group that the user is a member of, then the setting for the user is the setting that is applied. Consider this as indicating that the most user-centric setting is applied.

Restricting Login Times

A common example of a profile to set is restricting login times, or the times that users in an OS X environment are able to actually use a computer. To do so, open Profile Manager and click on the profile you wish to edit (in this example, we use a specific user who is playing with the computer past her bedtime). By default, login times are not managed with profiles, so click on Enable to enable managing printers (Figure 8-4).

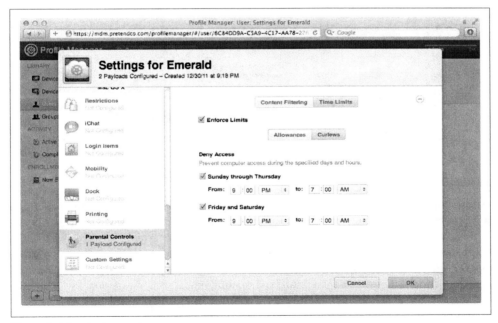

Figure 8-4. Login time options

Pushing Out Printers

Restricting login times is a common example of a restriction that can be set with Profile Manager. But the real power of profiles is automating aspects of pushing new users or computers out. A great example of this is pushing out new printers to users. Doing so with profiles does come with a caveat: the printer driver. First we'll look at pushing out a new printer. To do so, open Profile Manager and click on the profile you wish to edit (in this example, we use a specific user). By default, printing is not managed with profiles, so click on Enable to enable managing printers (Figure 8-5).

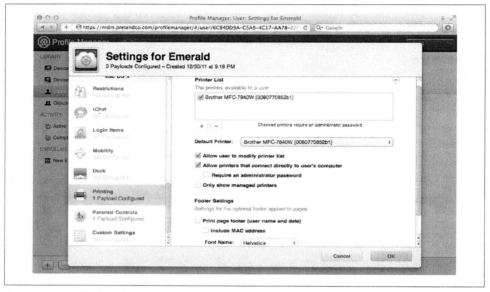

Figure 8-5. Profile-based printer deployment

Pushing Out New Dock Items

Another aspect of leveraging a profile to automate user and computer setup is pushing a dock item to users. For example, if you have Keynote installed on computers, you can use a profile to drop pages into the dock of each user. In this example, we're going to push a dock item for a group of users called "Marketing" for Keynote. To get started, open Profile Manager and click on the profile you wish to edit (in this example, we will use the Marketing group). By default, the dock is not managed with profiles, so click on Dock in the Settings sidebar and then click on Configure to enable managing docks (Figure 8-6).

You will then see the Display settings. Here, there are options to change the size of the dock, magnification options, location, and other settings. To add an item to the dock of managed clients, click on the plus sign ("+") and then select Keynote from the list of available applications, as seen in Figure 8-7. Once selected, click on Done to move on to other settings.

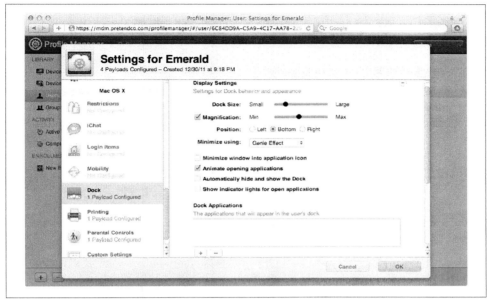

Figure 8-6. Managing the dock

Figure 8-7. Adding Keynote to a client's dock

Once applied, the Dock on managed clients will have Keynote. There is a Merge with User's Dock checkbox. When this option is checked (which is the default), the items in a user's dock will stay and any additional items from the profile will be added. When the merge option is disabled, the items in a user's dock will be removed and only the items in the profile will be displayed.

Setting Up Mail, Contacts and Calendars

One of the most useful aspects of configuration profiles is the ability to set up the user environment for Mail, Contacts, and Calendars to access your environment. When you are configuring such settings, you will first want to have the relevant information for accessing these services handy (each is covered in this book, if you are using a Mac OS X Server to provide these services). To configure Mail, open a profile and then click on Email in the left profiles sidebar (unless you are installing an Exchange account, in which case you should likely be using the Exchange settings). At the Configure Email screen, click on Configure.

At the Mail configuration screen, fill out the settings as you would with an email client, according to your setup.

If the User Name and Password fields are left blank, then the user will be prompted for her username and password when she installs the profile. Once the settings are configured appropriately for both incoming and outgoing mail, click on the OK button.

To configure the Calendar, click on the CalDAV option in the Settings sidebar and then click on the Configure button, as with other profile settings. At the configurations screen, provide the settings as you would for a client computer. In we show the settings for a server called calendar.krypted.com and the same username as was previously used.

Once the settings are configured appropriately for the Calendar client in iOS, click on the OK button to save the changes to the profile. Then click on CardDAV to configure the Address Book client. Here, provide the settings as you would with the client on a computer, clicking on OK when they have been appropriately configured.

In each of the previous examples, we only configured one connection to mail, contacts and calendars. However, it is worth noting that you can configure multiple accounts for each using the plus sign in the upper-right corner of the settings for that category.

Distributing Profiles

Now that you have built a bunch of profiles and settings, it is time to distribute them. The easiest way to distribute profiles is to have a user tap on them from within the client portal of Profile Manager. The client portal is different from the administrative portal, and typically made available to all users of the server. The client portal, known as MyDevices, is available at the address of the server with a /mydevices folder at the end. For example, if the portal is available at *https://mdm.krypted.com*, then you would access the client portal at *https://mdm.krypted.com/mydevices*.

Because users who have enrolled in Profile Manager are able to lock, wipe, and do other powerful tasks to their devices, the MyDevices portal is by default protected with the SSL certificate used to secure the Profile Manager service. When accessing the portal for the first time, users may be asked to accept the certificate if it is self-signed (see Chapter 2 for more information on SSL).

To enroll a device, first open the web portal from the device. Once open, authenticate when prompted (as you can see in Figure 8-8), using a username and password combination with access to the Profile Manager service.

Figure 8-8. Enrolling in Profile Manager

Once authenticated, you will see two tabs. The first tab, Devices, shows any devices enrolled by that user. Enrollment configures the device for Mobile Device Management. Updates sent via Mobile Device Management are instantly delivered to the device. The second tab, Profiles, shows all of the profiles available to the user that authenticated when prompted. To begin device enrollment, first click on Profiles.

From the Profiles tab, click (or tap) on any profile to begin the installation process for that profile. If you are enrolling the device for MDM, the Trust Profile for the server must first be installed. Tap on Install to install that profile, as seen in Figure 8-9.

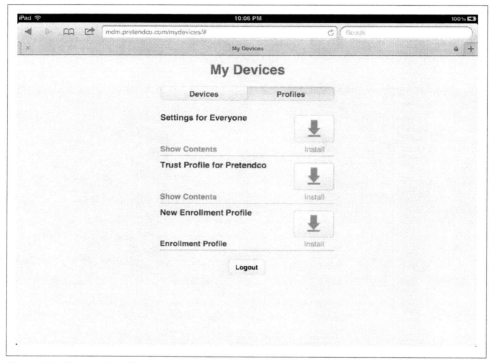

Figure 8-9. Trusting Profile Manager

Once installed, click or tap back on the Devices tab. Click on Enroll and the device will then prompt with the same screens as with the Profile installation. Once the device has been enrolled, the options to Wipe (erase all contents by revoking the encryption key) and Lock will be available (in Lion, this requires FileVault and a Recovery Partition whereas in iOS-based devices these options are built in). Additionally, controlling the device can now be done from within the Profile Manager web portal, as shown previously in this section.

Another way to distribute profiles is to save them from Profile Manager and then email them or use a website to distribute them without the Profile Manager component. To save the profile files, open the Profile Manager web interface. Then, choose a profile that you would like to export to a file. In the Profile tab for the profile, click on the Download button (Figure 8-10).

Figure 8-10. Downloading a profile

The Profile immediately downloads and starts the installation process. If you are installing the profile on the client you are downloading the profile from, then you can click through the installation process. Otherwise, cancel and then the Profile will be saved in the Downloads directory for the user who you are logged in as. Once downloaded, Profiles can be edited, emailed, or installed through custom web interfaces.

Managed Preferences

Managed Preferences is one of the many options available in Open Directory. Using Managed Preferences, administrators push settings to client computers that have been bound to the Open Directory environment. Open Directory uses various fields, or attributes, located within its database to push those settings out. That database is an LDAP database, the same type of database available in practically every modern implementation of a directory service to date.

 For more on setting up Open Directory itself and binding client systems to Open Directory, see Chapter 2.

A great example of using Managed Preferences is the parental controls options for a local computer running Mac OS X. If you open System Preferences from the Apple menu and click on the Users & Groups System Preference pane, you will see a list of the users on the local computer. Click on a nonadministrative user, and check the "Enable parental controls" checkbox to manage the account locally.

Once checked, click on the Open Parental Controls... button to bring up the Parental Controls System Preference pane. Here, you can enable the Simple Finder (a simplified user experience), limit which applications the user is able to open, edit whether the user can change their Dock, restrict access to websites, restrict access to manage printers, restrict burning optical disks, limit with whom the user can mail or chat, and restrict the use of computer to specific times (Figure 8-11). This is done per computer, per user, on a case-by-case basis. Managed Preferences leverages the same technology, but provides a means to control practically any setting on the system and to do so from a centralized server, for users and computers, or using groups of either.

Figure 8-11. Managing parental controls

These Managed Preferences are best controlled in Workgroup Manager. Open Workgroup Manager from */Applications/Server* and then login to the Open Directory environment. Once authenticated, click on a group of users and then click on the Preferences icon in the Workgroup Manager toolbar, to bring up the Managed Preferences screen.

The Managed Preferences screen is different for users and computers (or groups of either). The preferences available for users include:

Applications
Controls access to applications, Dashboard widgets, and Front Row

Classic
Allows access to the Classic environment (only applicable for OS 9 users)

Dock
Configures the look and contents of the Dock

Finder
Manages the preferences, options, and appearance of the Finder

Login
Most options are only available for Computers, but can control automated mounts and login items

Media Access
Limit access to mounted volumes (optical drives, FireWire, and USB-based volumes)

Mobility
Control mobile accounts and portable home directories

Network
Manage proxy information and, at the computer level, sharing preferences

Parental Controls
Centrally manage parental controls options

Printing
Centrally deploy printers

Software Update
Deploy Software Update Server settings

System Preferences
Limit access to System Preference panes

Universal Access
Controls accessibility options (e.g., those available for the hearing and sight impaired)

The traditional example everyone tends to use is managing the Dock. This preference is easy to configure and even more easily displayed in a screen shot (look Ma, the Dock switched to a different side of the screen). Therefore, we're going to show you how to do something a bit more useful instead: managing the Software Update Server (which we will then show you how to set up in the next section of this chapter). To do so, click on the Software Update option and click on the Always radio button (Figure 8-12).

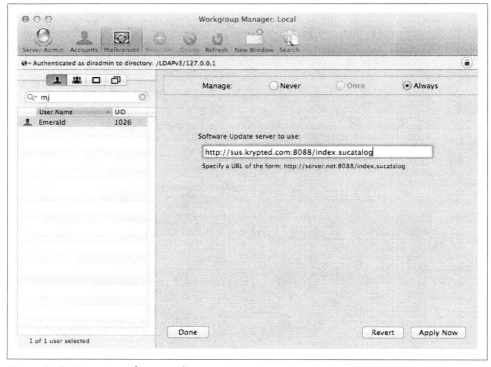

Figure 8-12. Managing software update

The Software Update preference only has one field. Click in the field and type the address of the server, with an http:// in front of it and a :8088/index.sucatalog at the end. Then click Apply Now. Logging into a client computer as a user who is a member of the group then shows that the client is trying to use the newly entered Software Update Server (note the title bar).

Of course, using the newly configured Software Update server will fail. But we'll get that configured in the next section (or change it back if you do not wish to manage that option). For now, go through each of the Managed Preference panes and explore which options, if any that you would like to centrally manage.

 Because Managed Preferences is built on the powerful LDAP protocol, the options available in Workgroup Manager can also be applied in environments leveraging other directory servers, such as Microsoft's Active Directory and various open source OpenLDAP implementations.

Software Update Services

Software Update is a service likely best suited for environments with at least five Mac OS X computers who are looking to centrally manage the software patches from Apple. These updates are cached on the Mac OS X Server and then deployed as needed to client systems that subscribe to the Software Update service installed on the server. This reduces the amount of bandwidth required on the server and allows administrators to release software in batches, thus keeping support costs at a minimum (assuming of course that most support incidents derive from change introduced in the environment).

Installing Software Update Server

The initial installation of Lion Server's Software Update service is one of the easier services to set up and manage. Begin by opening Server Admin and clicking on the name of the server you wish to install the Software Update service from the SERVERS list. Then click on the Settings button in the toolbar and click on the Services tab. Here, check the box for Software Update and click on the Save button.

Once the Service is listed under the name of the server in the SERVERS sidebar, click on Software Update there. No options need to be enabled in order for the Lion to be able to cache updates. However, given that it doesn't automatically cache any of the updates, some of these options on this screen can be useful. These include:

Limit user bandwidth to
> Throttles bandwidth on the server for software updates, useful with slightly larger environments

Store Updates in
> Specifies a directory to put software updates into (can type the path or use the Choose button to browse to the directory)

Provide updates using port
> Specifies the port number (the 8088 portion of the section "Managed Preferences" on page 155)

Copy updates from Apple
> If enabled, automatically caches updates (with an option for new versus all) to the server but does not enable them for client access

Automatically enable copied updates
> If enabled, automatically enables all of the updates copied locally in the previous option

Delete outdated software updates
> Removes old versions when a newer patch for that software title is available, conserving space

If you just want to mirror what Apple does with its software update and you don't want to control any options, check the box for Copy All updates from Apple and Automatically enable copied updates, leaving the other options the same.

Once configured as appropriate for your environment, click on the Save button. Then wait. The server will be a bit unstable while it's calculating what goes where and caching all these patches. I usually let them sit overnight. By the time I come back the next morning, I can start managing individual updates if I so desire.

Choosing Which Updates to Release

Managing each update can be tedious. The Software Update service is designed in such a way to make the process as streamlined as it can be. But Software Update management is not an easy topic. Picking which updates to release is tricky. Most will be simple and should be run following a cooling off period. Environments with few software titles and simple environments frequently have no cooling off period. Larger environments maintain cooling off periods between two weeks and years. Choose the one that works the best with your organization's security and patch management policy, if you have one.

The technical aspects of choosing the updates to enable is by far the easiest part of managing patches for OS X clients. From within Server Admin, click on the Software Update service in the SERVERS list. From here, click on Server Updates button in the Server Admin toolbar and you will see a list of all available software updates, as in Figure 8-13. Check the box for each to enable them.

Once enabled, running the Software Update application on each client will net them installing the updates enabled.

Configuring Clients

Mac OS X clients can be configured through the Software Update Managed Preference. But the clients can also be configured using the command line on each client system, if you do not wish to use Managed Preferences for other options. To configure the clients, use the defaults command, along with the write verb, to */Library/Preferences/com.apple.SoftwareUpdate*. The CatalogURL key is where the Software Update application takes its queue for software updates, which is then followed by the actual name or IP address of the server, port number and index.sucatalog, as follows:

```
defaults write /Library/Preferences/com.apple.SoftwareUpdate
    CatalogURL http://su.domain_name.com:8088/index.sucatalog
```

As mentioned previously, you can also use the options available in Workgroup Manager, to push out a managed preference or Profile Manager to push out a profile with the managed settings in the profile.

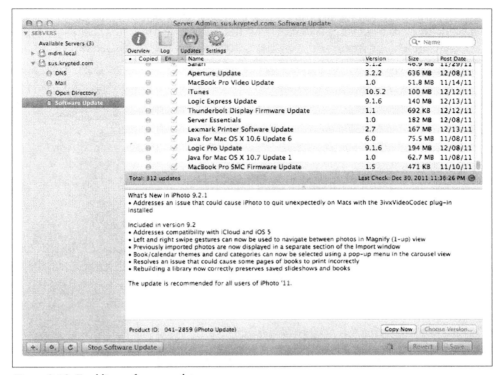

Figure 8-13. Enabling software updates

Conclusion

The centralized command and control of OS X clients is straightforward, and Apple has made it about as easy as it can be to use. However, centrally managing computers and iOS devices is a complicated task. Doing so should not be undertaken lightly, much as the decision to walk between multiple computers and change settings isn't undertaken lightly in large environments.

Most existing, large environments will already use Managed Preferences. Doing so is also a straightforward process, as we showed in this chapter. And setting up an Open Directory environment from scratch is fairly straightforward as well, as shown in Chapter 2. The hard part is determining a strategy that works best for you. If you have a small number of devices, just manage the settings on each individually or using a single group. However, if you have a lot of devices (as in 50,000 or more), then you should definitely consider the book *Enterprise Mac Managed Preferences* by Ed Marczak and Greg Neagle (Apress).

Managing profiles though is an entirely new paradigm. Profiles control managed preferences without a centralized directory service, but go further in layering actual device management on top. This device management gives administrators the ability to lock and even wipe devices from a centralized location. This is the future of centralized command and control of Apple devices, but not quite as mature today as that of Managed Preferences. For smaller environments though, it is probably preferable.

And of course, the Software Update Service gives that final piece of the puzzle, centralizing the ability to deploy patches to Mac OS X computers, including Lion and even Lion Servers. These options can then be deployed with the Managed Preferences or Profiles framework. But our use of Lion Server for the coolest of the cool doesn't end here.

CHAPTER 9

Network Services

Few servers come without the option to manage various services that most networks require. Lion Server is no exception to this rule. Most networks need network traffic routed into and out of the local network, services that automatically configure network settings for clients and DNS servers, useful for connecting to names of devices rather than IP addresses. These days, many also need to share usernames and passwords with third-party routers and firewalls and to provide secure connectivity to users when they are not on the local network (e.g., connecting to work from home).

Lion Server can provide all of these services. In this chapter, we'll look at a basic implementation of each service, how to configure clients (if appropriate), and more importantly when to and when not to use Lion Server's implementation of services and when to instead use something else.

When to Use Apple's Network Services

Each network service is one small part of what a Lion Server can do. Each is also a role that could live on entire clusters of servers in very large environments. If any of these services are mission critical for your environment, then you probably don't want them to run on a Lion Server. But if you're trying to establish an inexpensive means of connecting to your home network to keep the WebDAV connection from being published to the world or if you're trying to hand out more IP addresses than what an AirPort can do, a Mac OS X Server might be able to do the trick.

Overall, I would never recommend that anyone use the NAT service in Lion Server. A consumer-level appliance (which typically costs less than $100) can do a better job of acting as a gateway than an OS X Server. These devices give administrators far more options to manage incoming ports and usually have features that make the gateway far more usable.

Names are important in most networks, with Mac OS X Server being heavily reliant on DNS. Therefore, DNS gets used a lot. But DNS services are best left to internal DNS. Although OS X Servers can act as public DNS, public DNS is often better served from a registrar (e.g., Network Solutions) or a specialized DNS service (e.g., ZoneEdit). Having said this, managing DNS on a local network is something that a Lion Server is perfectly capable of doing.

VPN services for a few users are one place where a Lion Server can excel. Many consumer level devices are capable of passing VPN traffic. OS X Servers can act as a VPN Server and offer many of the same security features as other VPN servers. However, the ability to have a single repository for usernames and passwords is a great feature. Additionally, if you are using an Apple AirPort base station as your gateway appliance, OS X Server can automatically configure the device to open ports and configure the network in such a way that the VPN service just works, a great option for people that don't have the time or inclination to open ports for VPNs.

DHCP services for smaller subnets (e.g., less than 50 users) can be run on a gateway appliance or an OS X Server with about the same features being provided to client systems. But OS X Server has the ability to provide DHCP options that aren't available on most consumer routers, meaning that if you have specialized needs for DHCP options, a Mac OS X Server is a good fit for many environments.

Finally, many enterprises rely heavily on network services. For example, if the DHCP server goes down, users will not be able to access services from servers, resulting in many thinking that the "network is down." Also, when remote workers cannot access the network through a VPN, they cannot work, representing the potential for a lot of people to lose a considerable amount of productivity. The NAT and DNS features for very large environments (usually more than 150 people) in OS X Server are just not appropriate uses of resources.

Setting Up a VPN Server

The network service most commonly used on a Lion Server is VPN. This can be seen by the fact that the VPN service can be managed through the Server application. Setting up the VPN service can be done in about two or three minutes, and as mentioned previously, if you have an Apple AirPort acting as the gateway for the environment, the VPN service automatically opens ports into the server.

VPN is short for Virtual Private Network. A VPN is a tunnel that allows interconnecting two insecure networks by establishing a discreet channel between them. There are site-to-site VPNs that connect two entire networks, but this is the type of feature typically best left for VPN appliances, such as those by Cisco or SonicWALL. For the VPN services in Lion Server, we will only be looking at L2TP, or the Layer 2 Tunneling Protocol.

The L2TP server is simple to configure. Simply open the Server application and then click on the VPN service in the SERVICES section of the Server sidebar. Here, you will see three fields, as seen in Figure 9-1. The Shared Secret is a second password used for client systems. You will also have two fields for "Assign addresses between," which act as the first and last IP address dynamically handed out to clients who connect to the VPN. The Shared Secret will need to be provided to all VPN users and acts as a second factor in authenticating users (if the client doesn't have the correct Shared Secret then the username and password will not be submitted to the server). The IP addresses that are provided to clients should not conflict with any other DHCP scopes in use in the network (more on DHCP in the next section).

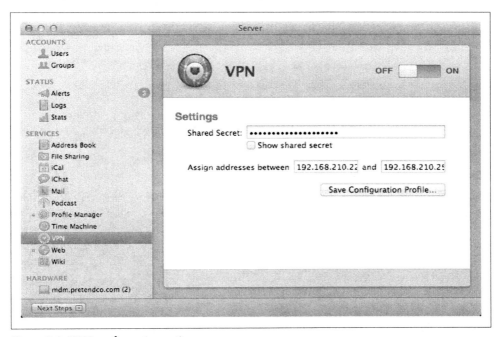

Figure 9-1. VPN configuration options

Once you have provided the Shared Secret and the IP addresses to be used by clients, use the ON and OFF switch to enable the L2TP service and the service will start, showing a green light (or jelly in Apple's terminology) beside the service once started.

Configuring the Network

Once enabled, you will need to open a few ports on your firewall. These include 500 (UDP), 1701 (UDP), 4500 (UDP), and 1723 (TCP). These should all be directed from the firewall, or gateway, to the IP address of the server. Once configured, you can use a port scanner, such as that available within Mac OS X's Network Utility to test the availability of ports. In Figure 9-2 we look at testing port 1723 for the IP address of a server from a remote location.

Many client systems will also use DNS to connect to the VPN server. If this is the case, then the public DNS will need to direct VPN clients to the public address of the gateway.

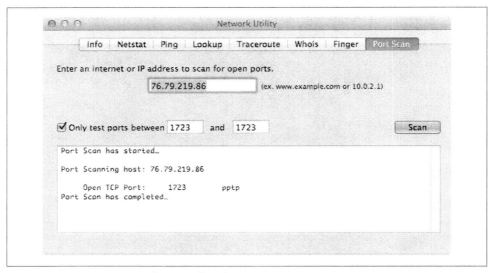

Figure 9-2. Scanning ports with Network Utility

For example, if you have a firewall configured on a public IP address, then the DNS name will need to point to the IP address of the firewall, which then routes incoming connections for the forwarded ports to the server. You can have multiple names for each IP address, and so to help future-proof your environment, it is often a good idea to configure a record for let's say vpn.krypted.com as well as another for calendar.krypted.com. This helps keep internal traffic routing to multiple servers even if they appear as one server from outside of your local network.

Finally, you will need to make sure that each user who you want to have VPN access has permissions to access the VPN. To do so, open the Server application and click on any user. Then click on the cogwheel icon toward the bottom of the screen and select Edit Access to Services... from the options shown. At the Service Access screen, check the box for VPN if it has not already been selected for the user account and click on the OK button to save your changes to the user's account.

You can select multiple accounts at the same time by holding down the Command key while clicking on user accounts and add access to the VPN service for all of them concurrently.

Setting Up the L2TP Clients

Once incoming connections are able to reach the server, it is time to configure clients. In this section, we will look at configuring an iPad and a Mac OS X client to connect to the VPN service. The iPad will have fewer options (e.g., cannot have a static IP address, subnet mask, or gateway setting) and so relies more heavily on the VPN service to be configured properly.

Connecting iOS-Based Devices

To configure the L2TP client on an iPad (or any other iOS-based device), open the Settings application on the device and then tap on General in the Settings sidebar. Next, tape on Network and then tap on VPN. Tap Add VPN Configuration... to create a new VPN connection.

Figure 9-3. Configuring the VPN client for iPad

At the Add Configuration screen (Figure 9-3), provide the following settings:

Description
  A description so users know what connection they are using (e.g., work or home VPN)

Server
  The IP address or DNS name of the server

Account
  The username used on the server

RSA SecurID
  Only use this option if you have a VPN that leverages an RSA SecurID token

Password
    The user's password

Secret
    The Shared Secret provided when the VPN service was enabled

Send All Traffic
    Routes all traffic going out of the iPad through the VPN tunnel, including traffic destined for the Internet that doesn't necessarily need to route through the VPN; for most environments, it is fine to disable this option to keep the amount of traffic coming into the network at a minimum

Proxy
    Use the proxy settings to provide a proxy server (e.g., a Squid server) if you are using one; otherwise leave the Proxy set to Off

Tap Save when you have configured the L2TP options and you will then see the new VPN connection in the Choose a Configuration... list. If the Configuration is checked, then use the ON and OFF switch in the VPN screen to enable or disable the VPN connection.

Provided that the VPN connection is established properly, the Status button will show that it has been connected and display how long the connection has been established for. Tapping on the connection then shows the public IP address of the VPN service in the Server field, the time connected in the Connect Time field, the LAN IP address of the VPN server in the Connected to field, and the IP address that is given to the client in the IP Address field of the Status screen.

Connecting Mac OS X-Based Devices

Practically any computer can connect to the L2TP service in Lion Server, including Mac OS X-based computers. While configuring iOS clients has little in the way of advanced features, Mac OS X VPN clients have a number of advanced features, including the ability to statically assign IP addresses and DNS servers.

To connect a Mac OS X computer to the VPN service, open the System Preferences (available under the Apple menu from any screen in Lion). Click on Network to bring up the Network System Preference pane.

At the resultant pop-up menu, select VPN in the Interface field and then L2TP over IPSec in the VPN Type field. Provide a name that makes it easier for whomever will use the interface to connect to the system (such as Krypted.com VPN in Figure 9-4). Click on the Create button to go to the new L2TP interface.

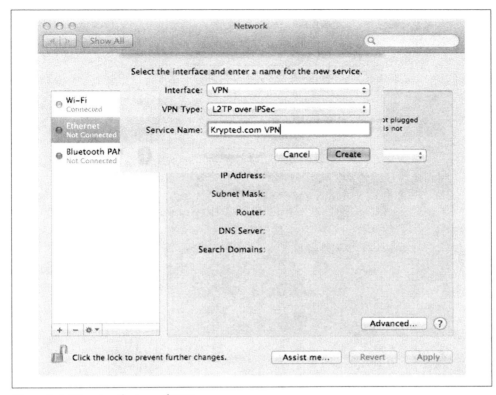

Figure 9-4. Choosing the type of VPN

From the newly created entry (Krypted.com VPN in Figure 9-5), provide the public IP address or DNS name of the Lion Server in the Server Address field and the username that was created in the Server application in the Account Name field.

Then click on the Authentication Settings... button to bring up the Authentication screen (Figure 9-6). Here, provide the user's password in the Password field and the Shared Secret from the Server application in the Shared Secret field, clicking on the OK button when you are finished.

 There are a number of other options in the Authentication screen that allow you to configure Kerberos, certificates, and various two factor authentication options. These are not by default configured with Lion Server as a VPN Server option; however, in order for connections to be established on demand, one of these options may be required. In the event that a non-Lion Server based VPN is being used and one of these options is required, see your network administrator for tips on configuring these options.

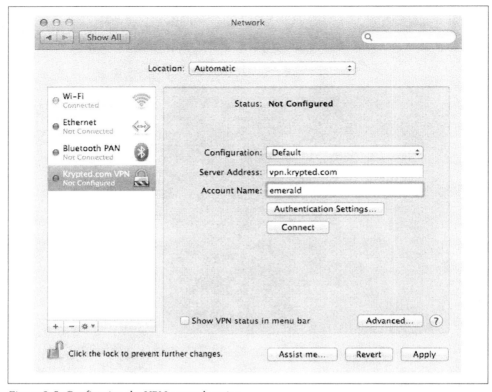

Figure 9-5. Configuring the VPN server location

At the main screen for configuring the VPN connection (Figure 9-6), click on Advanced to bring up a number of options, which are as follows (Figure 9-7):

Options

Configure disconnect times, whether all traffic runs over the VPN and logging options

VPN on Demand

Enables the VPN attempting to access a network resource accessed through the VPN tunnel

TCP/IP

Configure static IP addresses, gateways and subnet masks

DNS

The VPN client should automatically obtain a DNS server when connecting to the Lion Server's VPN service; however, you can also manually configure the DNS server or Search Domains (which are not provided by the VPN service automatically) using this screen

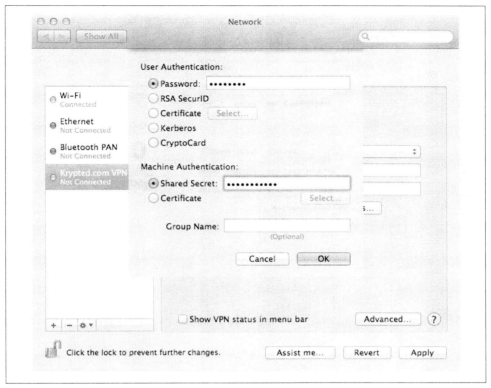

Figure 9-6. Configuring the connection credentials

Proxies

Allows administrators to configure proxy settings for clients. We don't cover proxies in this book, but many larger environments use them to secure various types of traffic and reduce network overhead of their connection to the Internet; if your environment requires a proxy to be configured request the appropriate settings to use here from your network administrators

The final option to cover is one of the most useful. At the main configuration screen for the VPN connection, there is an option to Show VPN status in menu bar. Using this option, users can click on a VPN icon in the upper-right corner of the screen and automatically establish a connection to the VPN. This makes the VPN far more usable, as users don't have to use the System Preferences to access the connection. Additionally, configuring the VPN on Demand options to automatically establish connections to resources over the VPN can help to make it where users don't even know they're accessing a VPN other than the slight latency encountered when opening the initial VPN-based resource. This helps to further the security and usability of the VPN, making it a truly useful and secure service.

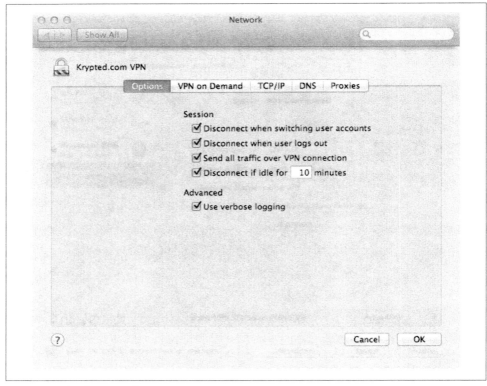

Figure 9-7. Configuring other VPN options

Sharing IP Addresses Using NAT

As mentioned earlier in this chapter, one of the least useful services in Lion Server is the Network Address Translation (NAT) service. Most Internet service providers (ISPs) supply you with one IP address. This address can then be used to put potentially thousands of computers on the same network using NAT, which then allows you to configure incoming connections to point at the server. These options are available in the Sharing System Preference pane on Lion computers until Lion Server is installed.

Once Server has been installed, use the Server Admin tool (available in */Applications/ Server*) to enable the service. To get started, open Server Admin and click on the name of the server in the SERVERS sidebar. Click on the Services tab and then check the box for NAT, clicking Save to show the NAT service under the server's name in the Server Admin sidebar.

Click on the NAT service and then click on Settings in the NAT toolbar. Here, you will see options to configure the NAT service. These include:

IP Forwarding only
> Creates a gateway without NAT (where the server is used to route traffic and all servers use public IP addresses); this is very rare and in the event that you are using this option, think very carefully about whether you should be

IP Forwarding and Network Address Translation
> Creates a gateway with NAT enabled; this option creates the traditional NAT connection used in practically every consumer-class router by default

External network interface
> Defines the network interface that will be the WAN (or Wide Area Network) connection; all other interfaces can then be used whereas their local network IP address is used on client computers to establish Internet connections (aka route network traffic outside of your Local Area Network (LAN)

If you're not really sure what to do, click on the Overview button and then click on the Gateway Setup Assistant. This will bring up a wizard that prompts you to select the WAN and LAN interfaces and then configure the service for you.

The most troublesome aspect of configuring NAT (other than the lack of features readily available on even a $40 LinkSys router) are the getting your WAN settings. In many cases, this can require considerable time spent on the phone with your ISP. In most cases, if you are using the NAT service, try to get what is referred to as a static IP address. One reason to do so is that (as we've mentioned several times throughout this book) Mac OS X Servers do not like to have their IP addresses change.

Hosting Your Own DNS

Mac OS X Servers also do not like their names to change. So much so that there is a hostname configuration wizard (described further in Chapter 2). DNS can be a holistic topic. This is because there are two views, arguably the public and private view. These are known as BIND views and each hostname can have different IP addresses associated to it based on which subnet that a request is made from.

In this section, we are only going to look at DNS on a local network, assuming that public-facing DNS is hosted on a public DNS server, such as those made readily available from Network Solutions and ZoneEdit. Because we are constraining our view of DNS (no pun intended) to the local network, it is worth starting off with the domain name you will be using. In this example, we will be using krypted.com. However, we could just as easily be using krypted.lan or krypted.home. In those cases, there would be no DNS available when you are outside the local network, unless using DNS over a VPN connection.

Because we are using krypted.com, we should also create records for any public services that are offered, mimicking the settings from the host for them (unless they are also hosted internally). For example, www.krypted.com is not located inside the network. Therefore, if we are using krypted.com, then we will need to define a www record externally in order to resolve that name internally (resolution is the response for a DNS record from the authoritative source). The server in this case is home.krypted.com. All external records for home.krypted.com and vpn.krypted.com are pointed to the public IP from outside of the environment. From inside, the same addresses point to the local server providing those services, allowing clients to connect without attempting to traverse the gateway for the network.

To get started, first set up the DNS service. To do so, open Server Admin and click on the name of the server in the SERVERS sidebar. Click on Settings in the Server Admin toolbar and then click on the Services tab. Check the box for DNS and click on Save to see the DNS service appear in the SERVERS list, below the name of the server.

Click on the DNS entry in the SERVERS list and then click on Zones in the Server Admin toolbar. In some cases, the server will automatically be listed. This happens when the server cannot properly resolve its own information. If the server is listed, then see Chapter 2 to resolve the issues that caused it to appear. Otherwise, click on Add Zone. There will be two options, Primary Zone and Slave Zone, as seen in Figure 9-8. A slave would automatically pull DNS records from the Primary, or Master. Click on Primary Zone to create your first domain that will be hosted on this DNS server.

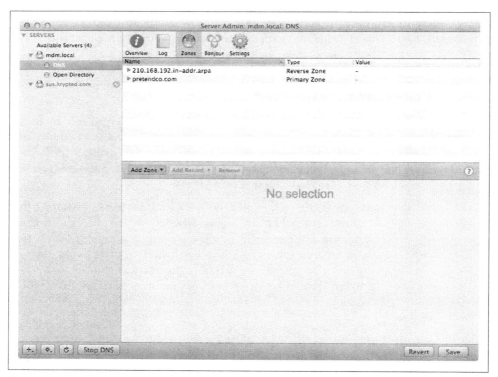

Figure 9-8. Configuring zones

When the new zone appears, click in the Primary Zone Name field and type the domain name that you are configuring (in this example, krypted.com as seen in Figure 9-9). Each domain requires an email address, which can be used in the event that there are problems with name resolution. In our example, we will use administrator@krypted.com. If there will be a slave, then also check the box for Allows zone transfer. Then use the plus sign ("+") to add a nameserver. When clicked, the name of the server you are configuring is automatically entered for the domain name provided in the Primary Zone Name field. If there will be mail then use the plus sign ("+") for the Mail Exchangers and provide the name of the mail server to use. Click on Save to create the zone, which in this case is the domain.

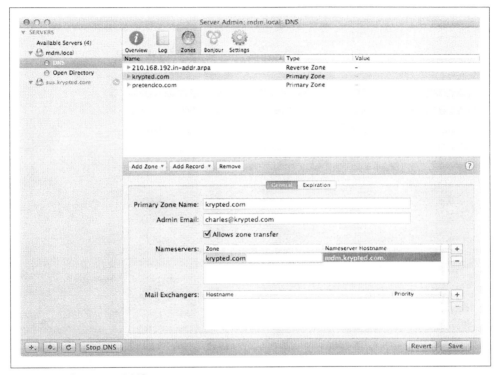

Figure 9-9. Creating a DNS zone

The zone is then created. Click on the name of the zone and then click on Add Record, selecting Add Machine (A) to create your first record for the domain. The only information required is the Machine Name and the IP Address of the machine. We are going to use home.krypted.com as the machine name (you should use the name of your server) and 192.168.210.250 as the IP address (you should use the IP address of your server), which can be seen in Figure 9-10. Click on the Save button to save these changes and if prompted, restart the DNS service.

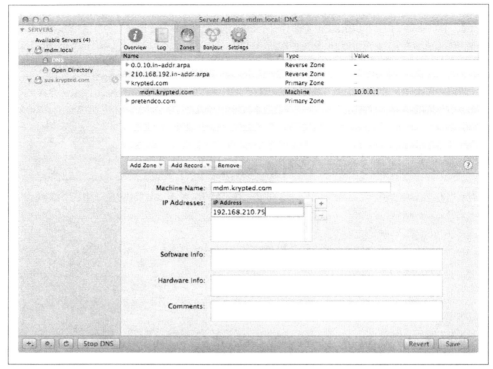

Figure 9-10. Creating an A Record

 Notice that a Reverse Zone has been created. This zone contains information about which name is authoritative for a given IP address. The reason this is so important is that forward and reverse information should match with what a server is configured to use.

Because we are also using the VPN service, we are going to create an alias record (also referred to as a CNAME) for the A record we just created. Click on Add Record and then select Add Alias (CNAME). You will then be prompted for an Alias Name and a Destination, as in Figure 9-11. These fields should be the name of the new record (vpn.krypted.com) and the record it will point to (home.krypted.com). Click on Save and restart the DNS service if prompted to do so.

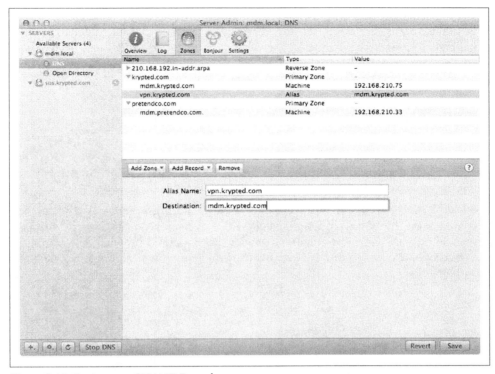

Figure 9-11. Setting up a CNAME Record

You have now configured a very simplistic DNS environment. Little further is actually supported in Mac OS X Server, aside from configuring slave servers to pull DNS information from the master server; however, for the needs of a smaller network environment, if a second server is needed, it would be easier to simply create the records from the master, given that there aren't likely to be many.

Configuring Wireless Access with RADIUS

RADIUS, short for Remote Authentication Dial-In User Service, is an authentication and accounting system used to share the usernames and passwords in a directory service to network devices. In this example, we will use RADIUS to provide usernames and passwords to an AirPort base station. The reason this example is so important is that it represents one case where Apple takes one of the more complicated technologies in the IT industry and makes it readily available to even non-network administrators. RADIUS also represents the highest level of security you can obtain when using Apple AirPort base stations.

You will need to be running a system that is either an Open Directory Master or Replica, or a system that is connected to a directory service in order to use RADIUS. For more on directory services, see Chapter 2. For this example, the AirPort will also need to have addresses configured and sit on the same network (preferably being accessible via Bonjour) that allow the server to connect to the base station.

Setting Up the AirPort

To get started, open Server Admin and click on the name of the server in the SERVERS sidebar. Click on Settings and then click on the Services tab. Check the box for RADIUS and then click the Save button to see the RADIUS entry appear below the server name in the Server Admin sidebar.

Click on RADIUS and then click on the Overview icon in the Server Admin toolbar. Here, click on the button to Configure RADIUS Service.... At the Server Certificate screen, choose the certificate that was previously configured (in Chapter 2) from the list of certificates available in the Certificate drop-down menu (Figure 9-12). Click on Continue.

Figure 9-12. Choosing a certificate

You will then see a list of available AirPort base stations. Click on the base station to configure to be managed by the server (in this example, we will be using krypted_RADIUS) and provide a password for the base station, as seen in Figure 9-13.

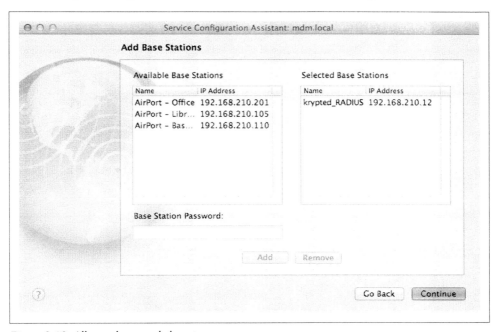

Figure 9-13. All your base are belong to us

Click on the Add button to place the AirPort in the righthand column, which shows the AirPorts that will be a part of the WPA2 Enterprise configuration created by the assistant. Once all of the AirPorts you want to configure have been added, click on the Continue button. At the Allowed Users screen, choose who can access the new wireless network. If you will not be granting wireless access to all of the users, it is usually best to have a dedicated RADIUS group for this purpose. For the purposes of this example, we will allow all of our users to access the wireless network, leaving the radio button set to "Allow all users," as in Figure 9-14. Click on Continue once you have configured the service as you see fit.

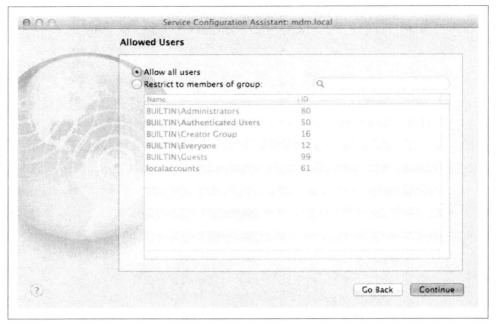

Figure 9-14. Configuring client access

At the Confirm RADIUS Settings screen, click on the Continue button and the settings will be written. The AirPort will then restart with the new settings applied for authenticating users.

Setting Up AirPort Clients

Once the AirPort has restarted, it will be shown by clicking on the list of available networks on a Mac OS X client computer. Click on it to bring up the username and password dialog box. Here, provide a username and password from the RADIUS server and click on the Join button.

If the server is using a certificate (by default, the assistant uses a certificate), and that certificate is self-signed (or otherwise untrusted by the client computer) then click on Show Certificate and make sure the "Always trust" checkbox has been checked (Figure 9-15). Provided the certificate is now trusted, click on the Continue button and authenticate to the local computer to accept the certificate.

The wireless network will then connect, provided you used a valid username and password combination from Open Directory. Once connected, the system will be joined to the wireless network and able to access services as with any other type of authentication mechanism used on an AirPort base station. The big difference is in the level of security that the wireless clients have to the server.

Figure 9-15. Trusting the certificate

Managing the Adaptive Firewall

Another security option in Lion Server is the adaptive firewall. In Lion Server, the adaptive firewall automatically blocks incoming connections that it considers to be dangerous. For example, if a client attempts too many incorrect logins, then a firewall rule restricts that user from attempting to communicate with the server for fifteen minutes. If you're troubleshooting and you accidentally tripped up one of these rules, then it can be a bit frustrating, which is why Apple gives us afctl, a tool that interacts with the adaptive firewall.

The most basic task you can do with the firewall is to disable all of the existing rules. To do so, simply run `afctl` (all afctl options require sudo) with a `-d` option:

```
afctl -d
```

When run, the adaptive firewall's rules are disabled. To re-enable them, use the `-e` option:

```
afctl -e
```

Turning off the rules seems a bit much for most troubleshooting tasks. To remove a specific IP address that has been blacklisted, use the `-r` option followed by the IP address (rules are enforced by IP):

```
afctl -r 192.168.210.88
```

To add an IP to the blacklist, use the `-a` option, also followed by the IP:

```
afctl -a 192.168.210.88
```

To permanently add a machine to the whitelist, use -w with the IP:

```
afctl -w 192.168.210.88
```

And to remove a machine from the whittles, use -x. To understand what is going on under the hood, consider this. The blacklisted computers are stored in plain text in /var/db/af/blacklist and the whitelisted computers are stored in the same path in a file called whitelist. The afctl binary itself is stored in /usr/libexec/afctl and the service is enabled by /System/Library/LaunchDaemons/com.apple.afctl.plist, meaning to stop the service outright, use launchctl:

```
launchctl unload com.apple.afctl.plist
```

Finally, the configuration file for afctl is at /etc/af.plist. Here you can change the path to the blacklist and whitelist files, change the interval with which it is run, and so on. Overall, the adaptive firewall is a nice little tool for Mac OS X Server security. Any good firewall that sits in front of Lion Server's firewall is a better tool for protecting systems, given that firewall appliances (even very inexpensive ones) will usually have features such as Stateful Packet Inspection that are capable of blocking far more issues than just incorrect password attempts.

Conclusion

The network services provided by Lion Server are not that great compared to other platforms and devices. DNS is capable to help resolve names on a local network. The VPN service is fine for smaller workgroups of users to connect to the network the Lion Server is on from remote locations. The RADIUS option is fine for AirPorts. The DHCP service can be used in smaller environments as well. If you have the budget to get a dedicated box to provide routing options, then the NAT service just shouldn't be used (we covered it for those who don't have such a budget).

But while the services are fine, they very much lack in scalability and modern features that most environments now rely on. Although far more complicated to use, if you find yourself needing more options for any of these services, then look to Microsoft Windows or Linux servers. However, for the target audience of this book, these services (other than NAT of course) should work for your needs. Now that we've covered building out a capable network environment, we'll put a heavy load on that environment in Chapter 10, when discussing imaging Mac OS X computers.

Deploying Mac OS X Computers

Deployment is the process for automating the configuration of new computers into a known state. Imaging is the process of placing an image on a computer, such as what Apple does prior to shipping new computers.

Deployment includes pushing an image to a client computer in a full fashion, a process known as monolithic imaging. But deployment can also mean a package-based workflow where you push out a minimal image and then lay automations on top of that image. Lion Server is an integral part of any imaging workflow.

In this chapter, we are looking primarily at the imaging aspect of deployment, appropriate for many small environments including homes and small offices. Lion is the first operating system from Apple deployed solely on the Internet. No more optical or USB media from Apple to install computers. This means that if you have a slow Internet connection that it can take a considerable amount of time to install new computers.

An example would be if you have 10 computers that you want to install from scratch. Each has to download the entire operating system over the Internet independently. Each also has to be configured to work on the network, log into the server and maybe have a few pieces of software installed as well. This entire process can take up to two hours per system. However, if you have an image that you have prepared, you can probably do all 10 computers within 20 minutes or less, with the systems completely configured and a perfect uniform configuration between them.

The Basics of Imaging Mac OS X

Imaging is a process where a client computer boots to a disk and performs a data restoration to another disk. You cannot image a drive that you are booted to, as doing so would mean erasing your boot volume. Therefore, when imaging Mac OS X client computers, you need to boot to one place and image another. This can mean rebooting your computer through Target Disk Mode and then using a program such as Carbon Copy Cloner to clone files, or a logical set of files in a bundle known as an image, to the computers. This can also meaning to a boot volume hosted on a network using Apple's NetBoot technology.

NetBoot is a tool for booting from an image on a server. Once booted, Apple has two options for deployment. The first is known as NetInstall, which performs an installation on client systems, along with a number of automations customized to that system. The second is known as NetRestore, which takes an image and restores it to a volume in its entirety. All three require the development of images, done using a tool called System Image Utility, available in the */Applications/Server* directory of a computer that has had the Server Admin Tools installed (for more on installing the Server Admin Tools for Lion Server, see Chapter 2).

 In this chapter, we look at using Lion Server as a NetBoot server; however, there are third-party tools for performing such an operation.

When imaging there are a number of automations that need to occur to the data imaged in order to have that system be unique. In this chapter, we look at using a few different tools to make systems unique, including Disk Utility. However, it is worth noting that not all imaging tools actually make the system unique (e.g., SuperDuper!), as many are built for backup, not mature solutions for imaging multiple systems.

Imaging with Disk Utility

Before we cover imaging using the tools available in Lion Server, first it is most appropriate to look at imaging using tools available in all Mac OS X computers. In this case, we will look at imaging using Apple's Disk Utility, available in the */Applications* directory. In this example, we will take one drive (called source for ease of use), create an image of that drive, and then deploy the image to a second drive (called target, to keep things simple).

We can use Disk Utility to image one drive to another, as Disk Utility is capable of resetting the system to be somewhat unique but would still require a manual change to the computer name. To get started, first mount both the drive you will be imaging from (the source) and the drive you will be imaging to (the target) on the computer you will use (you should not use the source or the target as the computer to perform this task).

In order to help keep straight which system is which, rename either the source or the target to something easily memorable. Open Disk Utility and as you can see in Figure 10-1, we are using computer hard drives called source and target, as well as the boot volume of the system we are imaging with.

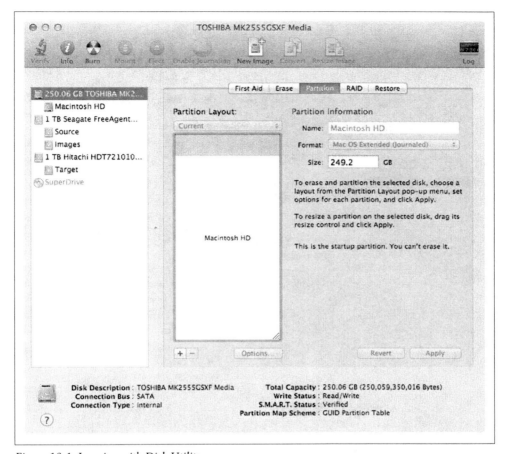

Figure 10-1. Imaging with Disk Utility

Before you do any restores of anything, make sure that you've backed up your systems and that there is no data on the targets, or destinations, that will be lost. These restores fully erase the targets, using the steps we provide.

Click on the target drive and then click on the Restore tab. Here, drag the name of the source volume into the Source field and the name of the target volume into the Destination field, as can be seen in Figure 10-2.

The Restore button will be highlighted once a volume has been placed in each field. Click on Restore and then wait. The process will take some time. Once complete, test booting to the volume that was restored to, and provided it boots appropriately, rename the computer and you have imaged your first machine!

You can also use this same process to create a compressed file (*.dmg*) that can then be restored to client systems as well. This is a good way to make a snapshot of a machine before running any installers on it, or to keep an image until it is needed for subsequent

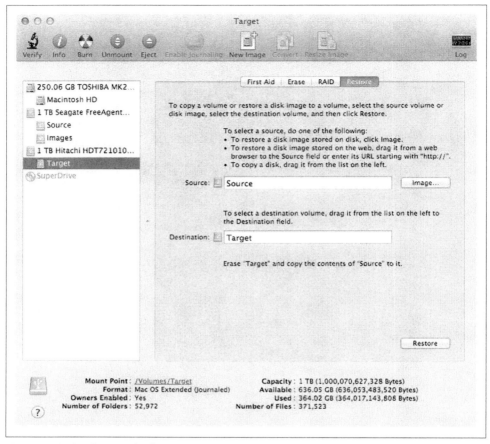

Figure 10-2. Configuring the destination

restores, without dedicating a drive to the image. To do so, open Disk Utility and click on the disk that will be your source for the image. Then, click on the File menu and click on New. Then, click on the Disk Image from disk0 (or whichever disk is listed for the volume you wish to create an image from) as can be seen in Figure 10-3.

Figure 10-3. Imaging from a .dmg file

Next, configure a few settings for the disk image that you are about to create. At the Save As screen, provide a name for the image and choose a location in the Where dialog box. Do not encrypt the image and leave the Image Format as compressed for this example, as seen in Figure 10-4.

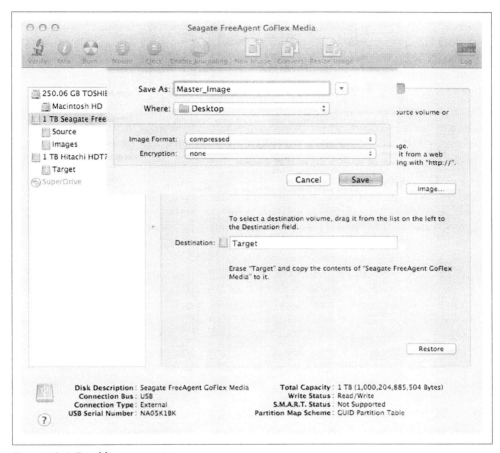

Figure 10-4. Disabling encryption

The image file can then be restored to a hard drive by dragging a target volume into the Destination field of a Restore screen and using the Image button by the Source field to browse for the image file. Compressed images take up much less space, but do take a bit longer to restore.

The whole concept of an image is the foundation for most imaging environments. In the next few sections, we'll use an image as an installer (NetInstall), as the restore for an imaging process that includes other installation automations (NetRestore), and as an operating system for client computers (NetBoot).

Using NetBoot

As was mentioned earlier in this chapter, NetBoot is used to boot a computer to an operating system that is hosted on a network. Lion Server has a NetBoot Service that is managed using Server Admin, located in */Applications/Server*. NetBoot has a few uses, including lab systems that boot from a lab server and imaging. The use for imaging is now the most prevalent use of NetBoot: because you don't want to image either your source or your target, you can NetBoot a client to image it, rather than use Target Disk Mode.

To use Lion Server's NetBoot Service, first create a NetBoot set. This is a disk image located inside a NetBoot bundle (a file with a *.nbi* extension). Once a NetBoot set has been created, it gets activated in Server Admin and voilà, you have a network-based operating system.

NetBoot has options for disabling various models of computers (you wouldn't want a G3 to try and boot off a Lion image after all), running diskless clients (great if you are so secure an environment that you don't believe in actually using hard drives—or if you own hats made of tin foil), and hosting multiple NetBoot images.

Building a NetBoot Set

The first step in configuring the NetBoot service is to create a NetBoot set. This is a disk image containing the operating system that is used to boot client computers to the Lion Server. To get started, first install a computer with an operating system that you want client systems to use. Then, boot that system to target disk mode and connect it to the server. Then open System Image Utility and click on the volume in target disk mode from the list of Sources. Click on NetBoot Image and then click on Continue.

At the Image Settings screen, provide the following (Figure 10-5):

Network Disk
> The name of the hard drive that is mounted for client computers

Description
> Enter a description for the image; usually it is a good idea to include software, versioning, and the date the image was created

Image will be served from more than one server
> Use this checkbox if you will have two (or more) NetBoot servers that both host this image

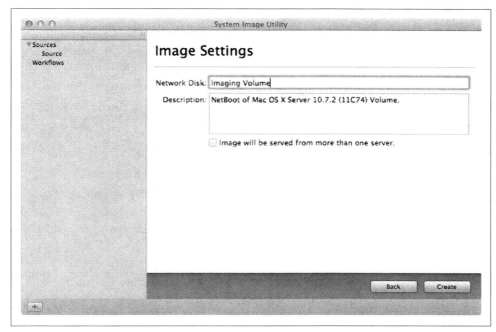

Figure 10-5. Selecting image settings

Click on Create once the settings are appropriate and then click on Agree to agree to the OS X licensing agreement from Apple (this is similar to clicking on Agree on each client that the Lion operating system is used on). When prompted for the location of the NetBoot set, select the Desktop or another location that you wish to keep the Net-Boot set.

You will then be prompted to provide an administrative username and password, and the image will be created. This can take a while, according to the size of the image, so run and get a cup of coffee and we'll pick up again in the next section.

Hosting a NetBoot Set

In the previous section, we looked at creating a NetBoot set. These are bundles with a *.nbi* extension, which contain all of the data required to boot a client computer to a network operating system. Once you have created a NetBoot set, you'll then want to configure the NetBoot service to host the network operating system. To get started, open Server Admin (from */Applications/Server*, provided you have the Lion Server Admin tools installed) and click on the name of the server you will be using. Then click on Settings and then click on the Services tab. Here, check the box for the NetBoot service and click on the Save button at the bottom of the screen.

The NetBoot service then appears under the name of the server in the SERVERS toolbar. Click on NetBoot and then check the box for Images and Client Data for the hard drive that the NetBoot image will live on (Macintosh HD in Figure 10-6). By default, the Ethernet interface is also selected (it is usually best to only run NetBoot on one network interface, not two).

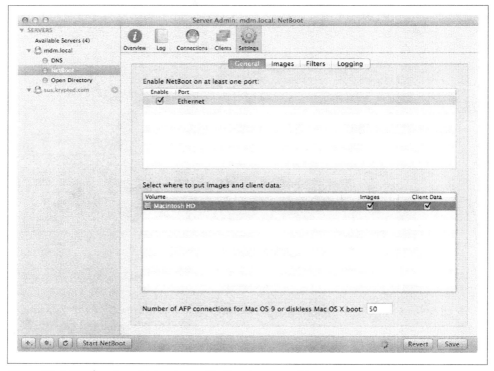

Figure 10-6. Configuring which volumes NetBoot images reside on

Once you have enabled the hard drive that will have a NetBoot image on it, click on Save. Then, the copy the NetBoot set created in the previous section to the *Library/NetBoot/NetBootSP0* directory of that volume. Provided that the copy completes properly, go back to Server Admin and click on NetBoot's Images tab. Here, you will then see the NetBoot image you just copied. Click on the checkbox for Enable and the radio button for Default as you can see in Figure 10-7, clicking Save and then Start NetBoot to complete the setup.

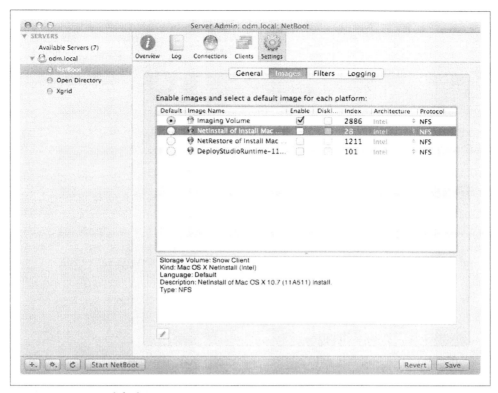

Figure 10-7. Setting default images

Using a NetBoot Client

Once the server is set up, you can then NetBoot client systems. In order for a client to NetBoot to the server, the client must have an IP address, subnet mask, and be on the same subnet as the server. If the client is not on the same subnet, then you can still connect using the bless command, or by setting up what is known as a NetBoot Helper.

But the easiest way to use a NetBoot client is to let the client system automatically find the NetBoot server. There are two ways to do so. The first is using the Startup Disk System Preference pane. When you click on Startup Disk from System Preferences (System Preferences is available under the Apple menu from any screen), any volumes that appear with a globe that has a green arrow below it indicate a network operating system. Clicking on it and clicking on Restart will reboot the system to that network volume.

You can also use the N key at startup to automatically look for the closest NetBoot server and boot from it. Booting holding down the Option key will produce a list of

NetBoot and local volumes. All of the options available still require the client computer to obtain an IP address automatically and be on the same subnet as the server.

The bless command is used to set the boot drive that a system will use. It comes with a nifty --netboot option. Define the server and (assuming you have one nbi) you can reset the boot drive by sending a Unix command through ARD:

```
bless --netboot --server bsdp://192.168.210.90
```

At the next restart of the computer, it will then automatically boot to the default image hosted on 192.168.210.90.

Using NetInstall

As mentioned earlier in the chapter, NetInstall is a tool used to create a custom installer of Mac OS X that is hosted from a centralized server. The NetInstall image, at creation time, will have a number of automations associated with it. These automations are capable of setting up network settings, installing software, renaming computers, and running scripts (which in turn gives unlimited potential to what can be done).

As with NetBoot, the first step with NetInstall is to build the image.

Building a NetInstall Image

To get started with building your NetInstall image, you will first need the Lion installer, available on the App Store. Once downloaded, you won't need to run the installer; instead, just leave it in the /Applications directory where it automatically downloads. You can also download it and then save the Install Mac OS X Lion installer on a hard drive, so that you can copy it to the /Applications directory of the system you will be running System Image Utility on. With the installer in your /Applications directory (therefore, before you actually install Lion), open System Image Utility.

Next, we'll create the Network Disk Image. When the Install Mac OS X Lion installer is in the /Applications directory, the option for NetInstall Image will be available when you open System Image Utility. Click on Install Mac OS X Lion in System Image Utility sidebar (under Sources) and then click on the radio button for NetInstall Image. Once NetInstall image has been clicked, click on the Continue button.

Next, customize the NetInstaller. At the Image Settings screen, provide the following information:

Network Disk
  The name of the hard drive that is mounted for client computers

Description
  Enter a description for the image; usually it is a good idea to include software, versioning and the date the image was created

Image will be served from more than one server
> Use this checkbox if you will have two (or more) NetBoot servers that both host this image

When you click on Create, the image will be created (as with a NetBoot image, you also need to agree to the licensing agreement and provide the username and password for a local administrator of the system you are creating the NetInstall image on). This image is just like having a network copy of the Mac OS X installer on your Local Area Network, which lets you install Lion systems faster.

Alternatively, you can also build in a number of powerful automations into the NetInstall image. In the following example, we will create a local workflow that creates a local administrative account. From System Image Utility, use the NetInstall option and then click on the Customize button instead of the Continue button before providing the settings for the image, which brings up a screen that resembles Automator, complete with an Automator Library specific to System Image Utility options (Figure 10-8).

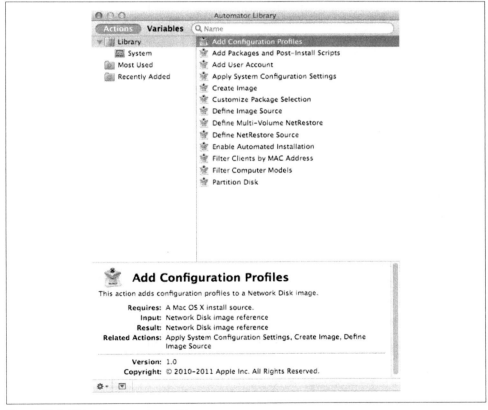

Figure 10-8. Using the Automator Library

By default, the Define Image Source workflow item will have the Install Mac OS X Lion image and there will be a Create Image workflow item with the same options that were available previously. Drag the Add User Account workflow item from the Library to between the Define Image Source and Create Image options. Notice that the workflow items are all then linked, as seen in Figure 10-9.

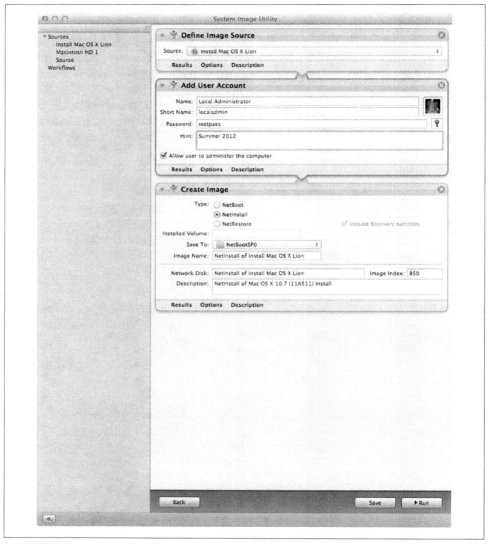

Figure 10-9. Customizing workflows

If the items are not linked, then the imaging process will not include any unlinked items.

Name

Provide a name for an administrator account that will be created on the NetBoot image

Short Name

Provide a short name for the above administrative account

Password

Enter the password that will be used on the administrative account created

Hint

A Password hint, used at the Login Window (e.g., summer 2012 if all of your systems purchased in the summer of 2012 have the same local administrative password)

Allow user to administer the computer

Adds the user account as an administrator (e.g., to the Administrators group)

The Save button is used to save a copy of the workflow on the computer you are imaging from. The workflow can then be imported into other Mac OS X computers and used to create images. You can also use the Run option to create the NetInstall image. You will be prompted to provide a local administrator's username and password and then the image will be created and placed into the location from the Save To option. If you have already set up the NetBoot service, as described previously in this chapter in the section "Using NetBoot" on page 188, the NetBootSP0 directory will be the default home for the image.

Once created, you can NetBoot a client to the server and it will automatically start the setup process for Lion on client systems. There are a number of other workflow items that can be added to a workflow, to be saved into an image. The Automator Library includes the following (in addition to the Add User Account):

Add Configuration Profiles

Installs Configuration Profiles on client systems (for more information on Configuration Profiles, see Chapter 8).

Add Packages and Post-Install Scripts

Runs a package installer (*.pkg* or *.mpkg*) or a shell script. Packages are typically distributed by software developers to aid you in installing their software (e.g., Microsoft). Scripts are one of the most powerful aspects of the imaging process, giving administrators access to change any setting on client systems.

Apply System Configuration Settings

Binds clients to a directory service, renames computers and resets ByHost settings (usually a good idea to check this box).

Create Image

Part of every workflow, specifies the name of the image and where it saves to when the workflow is run.

Customize Package Selection
>   Used to, for example, install the Server Software package.

Define Image Source
>   The installer or disk image (*.dmg*) or disk used for NetBoot and NetRestore options (for more on NetRestore, see the section "Deploying Computers with NetRestore" on page 196 later in this chapter).

Define Multi-Volume NetRestore
>   If you are using NetRestore, gives an option to restore one disk image per local volume on client computers.

Define NetRestore Source
>   Used to create a NetBoot set that restores NetRestore images over a network, such as those located on an AFP share or using multicast asr (asr is the command-line process used as the backend for most every imaging scenario in Mac OS X).

Enable Automated Installation
>   If a disk will get erased as part of the installation, enables administrators to automatically choose which disk and then choose a language for the installer to use, thus requiring less keystrokes during the installation process. This is a must for "1 touch deployments" where you boot a lot of computers holding down the N key and everything just images with no further input during the process.

Filter Clients by MAC Address
>   Enables you to define a number of MAC addresses that the image will install on, or to define MAC addresses that the image specifically will not install on.

Filter Computer Models
>   Enables you to define a number of computer models that the image will install on, or to define computer models that the image specifically will not install on.

Partition Disk
>   Used early in the workflow process, the Partition Disk option is used to split up hard drives in multivolume restores, or in the event that you want the operating system and user data to be separate from one another.

As you can see, there are powerful automations available for imaging. When we image 50,000 computers, these are a must. But when I image my wife's computer at home, I use a very basic and generic workflow. The options are built to allow scaling but not to require you to write complicated Python scripts and build crazy packages for every option you may use, whether you are using NetInstall or NetRestore.

Deploying Computers with NetRestore

NetInstall creates a network installer that runs over NetBoot. NetRestore is a bit different in that instead of running an operating system installer, you are actually pushing out an image. This prepared image usually has software and customizations within the image itself, often making the deployment simpler and/or faster. When using

NetRestore, you are going to fully erase the hard drive that you are restoring your image onto and once the image is restored possibly perform some minor automations. In this example, we will change the name of the computer and bind it to the Open Directory service running on our OS X Server as part of our imaging automation.

To get started, mount the drive that you want to build an image from via Target Disk Mode on a system running the Server Tools (can be the server if you like). Open System Image Utility and select the disk to use as the image from the Sources menu to bring up the Create a Network Disk Image screen. Click on NetRestore Image and then click on the Customize button.

Clicking on Continue instead of Customize will create an image with no customizations. However, since you should not have systems with duplicate names, we are going to change the name of the computer as a postflight imaging task.

Drag the Apply System Configuration Settings object from the Automator Library in between the Define Image Source and Create Image options. In the Apply System Configuration Settings workflow item, check the box for Connect computers to directory servers:. Here, provide the name of the Open Directory server as well as the administrative username and password used to create the directory service (e.g., diradmin) as you can see in Figure 10-10.

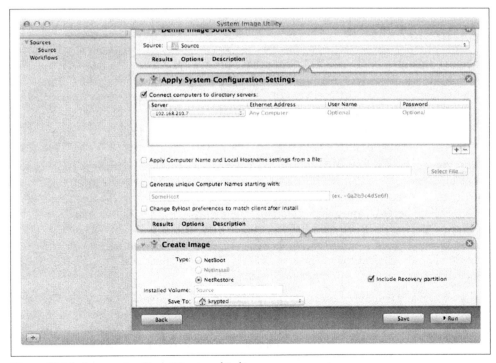

Figure 10-10. Automating Open Directory binding

Also check the box for "Generate unique computer names starting with" and enter a name you would like prefixed to all of your computer names used with this workflow (e.g., the acronym of your school's name, your family's last name, or the name of a business). Each computer imaged will then have the name you provide followed by a randomly generated name and each system will also be bound into your directory service, thus taking any managed preferences you define (for more on Managed Preferences, see Chapter 8).

Click Run to create the image and because it is saving to NetBootSP0 you would simply need to go to the NetBoot service within Server Admin and check the box for this image to enable it.

NetRestore is the more powerful of all the deployment options in OS X Server. However, as you have seen in this example, once we installed all the software on our image (that computer we are imaging the hard drive from is often referred to as a "golden master"), the process seems simple at first. However, by using an image with Windows 7 on it, a Recovery partition (described further in Chapter 2) and maybe another image with Linux, we can deploy three, four, or even more operating systems to each client. We can also overlay updates for packages installed in the base image using the Add Packages and Post-Install Scripts workflow item and perform all the same imaging tasks we could with NetInstall.

Conclusion

The imaging options in Mac OS X Server have not changed drastically in over 10 years. We have different names and different graphical elements that sit atop the foundations built by Apple even before the advent of Mac OS X: asr (short for Apple System Restore). NetBoot was one of the first options that Steve Jobs referenced when he first unveiled Mac OS X back in the days of 10.0. Now that we are on 10.7, Lion has an extremely mature set of imaging options in NetBoot, NetInstall, and NetRestore.

While the options in Lion are mature, there are other solutions that are even better for some environments. DeployStudio is a free imaging solution with far more logic built into it, and an easier deployment methodology. JAMF Software has the Casper Imaging Server, which helps to unify their patch management solution with the imaging process of client computers. If you are imaging a lot of computers, definitely check these out. While Lion Server is a perfectly ample solution for many environments, the other features available with DeployStudio and JAMF's Casper Imaging Server can save enough time to warrant using them instead!

Once systems are imaged, there are a number of other options to consider. Keeping software up-to-date is one of the top things that can be done to secure any computer. Keeping software up-to-date also makes using that software a much more pleasing experience. There are a number of solutions that help keep software up-to-date, such as Mac OS X Server's Software Update service (covered in Chapter 8) and Apple Remote

Desktop. Additionally, third-party vendors such as JAMF's Casper Suite, FileWave, Absolute Manage, and others can be used in large environments, where granular controls and policies are critical.

Finally, as with many other features throughout this book, imaging can be set up and configured in about 30 minutes or less. The more machines you have, the more options you will invariably need to use from Apple's plethora of options. However, don't overcomplicate the process. I would recommend starting simple, with basic NetInstall options and then, as you feel more complicated options are necessary, move up into the prepared images with NetRestore, using NetBoot as a foundation to manage both.

About the Author

Charles Edge, Jr. is the Chief Technology Officer at 318, a consultancy based out of Santa Monica, CA. While certified with Microsoft, Symantec, and others, Charles spends much of his time writing about and consulting on Mac OS X and iOS. Charles is the author of several books on OS X systems administration, including the *Enterprise Mac Administrator's Guide* and the *Enterprise iPhone and iPad Administrator's Guide* (both with Apress).

Charles speaks at conferences regularly, including MacWorld, MacIT, MacTech, Mac-SysAdmin, LinuxWorld, BlackHat, LayerOne, and DefCon. Charles also runs and maintains *http://www.krypted.com* in his spare time, a site dedicated to lucid systems administration.

Get even more for your money.

Join the O'Reilly Community, and register the O'Reilly books you own. It's free, and you'll get:

- $4.99 ebook upgrade offer
- 40% upgrade offer on O'Reilly print books
- Membership discounts on books and events
- Free lifetime updates to ebooks and videos
- Multiple ebook formats, DRM FREE
- Participation in the O'Reilly community
- Newsletters
- Account management
- 100% Satisfaction Guarantee

Signing up is easy:

1. **Go to: oreilly.com/go/register**
2. **Create an O'Reilly login.**
3. **Provide your address.**
4. **Register your books.**

Note: English-language books only

To order books online:

oreilly.com/store

For questions about products or an order:

orders@oreilly.com

To sign up to get topic-specific email announcements and/or news about upcoming books, conferences, special offers, and new technologies:

elists@oreilly.com

For technical questions about book content:

booktech@oreilly.com

To submit new book proposals to our editors:

proposals@oreilly.com

O'Reilly books are available in multiple DRM-free ebook formats. For more information:

oreilly.com/ebooks

O'REILLY®

Spreading the knowledge of innovators   oreilly.com

The information you need, when and where you need it.

With Safari Books Online, you can:

Access the contents of thousands of technology and business books

- Quickly search over 7000 books and certification guides
- Download whole books or chapters in PDF format, at no extra cost, to print or read on the go
- Copy and paste code
- Save up to 35% on O'Reilly print books
- **New!** Access mobile-friendly books directly from cell phones and mobile devices

Stay up-to-date on emerging topics before the books are published

- Get on-demand access to evolving manuscripts.
- Interact directly with authors of upcoming books

Explore thousands of hours of video on technology and design topics

- Learn from expert video tutorials
- Watch and replay recorded conference sessions

Spreading the knowledge of innovators   safari.oreilly.com

CPSIA information can be obtained at www.ICGtesting.com
Printed in the USA
BVOW080013290512

291252BV00003B/2/P